Introduction to subject indexing.
a programmed text

VOLUME II: UDC AND CHAIN
PROCEDURE IN SUBJECT CATALOGUING

A G Brown

IN COLLABORATION WITH D W LANGRIDGE & J MILLS

CLIVE BINGLEY
LONDON

LINNET BOOKS
HAMDEN · CONN

FIRST PUBLISHED IN THE UK 1976 BY CLIVE BINGLEY LTD
16 PEMBRIDGE ROAD LONDON W11 · SIMULTANEOUSLY PUBLISHE
IN THE USA BY LINNET BOOKS AN IMPRINT OF THE SHOE STRING
PRESS INC 995 SHERMAN AVENUE HAMDEN CONNECTICUT 06514.
SET IN 10 ON 12 POINT PRESS ROMAN
PRINTED AND BOUND IN THE UK BY REDWOOD BURN LTD
TROWBRIDGE AND ESHER · COPYRIGHT © A G BROWN 1976
ALL RIGHTS RESERVED · CLIVE BINGLEY ISBN: 0-85157-211-1
LINNET BOOKS ISBN: 0-208-01529-9

Library of Congress Cataloging in Publication Data

Brown, Alan George.
    An introduction to subject indexing.

    CONTENTS: v. 1. Subject analysis and practical
classification. — v. 2. UDC and chain procedure in
subject cataloguing.
    1. Subject cataloguing—Programmed instruction.
2. Indexing—Programmed instruction. I. Langridge,
Derek Wilton. II. Mills, Jack, 1918- III. Title.
Z695.B87   1976   025.3'3   75-33276
ISBN 0-208-01524-8 (v. 1)
ISBN 0-208-01529-9 (v. 2)

PREFACE

In the preface to Volume I we explained that the content of this programmed text is based upon work initially conducted under a research
project financed by the Office for Scientific and Technical Information
(now the British Library Research and Development Department) and
carried out at the School of Librarianship, the Polytechnic of North
London in co-operation with the College of Librarianship Wales.

We stated that our intention was to attempt to provide an integrated
view of some basic principles and practices of subject indexing rather
than imparting a high degree of familiarity with any particular system.
This statement applies, of course, to the present volume which must
therefore be seen as building directly upon the content of Volume 1.

Volume 1 is concerned with the subject analysis of documents, primarily
at the level of summarisation, and the process of translation into classification schemes. In this latter respect we utilised the 6th edition of the
Colon Classification as the vehicle for exemplification.

In Volume 2 we consider translation into UDC and the techniques of
chain procedure, based upon UDC, in the construction of the classified
and alphabetical subject catalogues. The text assumes a familiarity on
the part of the reader with the concepts dealt with in the earlier volume.
In particular, when dealing with practical classification by UDC, we
assume a familiarity with the concepts and procedures of subject analysis
and an appreciation of the system of Fundamental Categories upon which
analysis and synthesis within the Colon Classification is based.

In short, whereas Volume 1, the start of this course, assumes no prior
knowledge of classification or subject indexing on the part of the reader,
this second volume does. It is, however, our hope that, by so dividing
the text, a reader possessing the required background can regard this second
part as an entity in itself.

A G BROWN
School of Library, Archive and Information Studies
University College London
September 1975

NOTE

This is the second of two volumes dealing with practical classification and subject indexing. As such it presupposes a knowledge, on the part of the reader, of the concepts and practices dealt with in Volume 1. In particular the reader should have a familiarity with the following concepts. Such a familiarity will be assumed in the succeeding text.

1 Specific summarisation of the subject content of documents.

2 Distinctions between disciplines, phenomena, or objects of study, and form concepts.

3 Categories and facets.

4 The importance of citation order in classification.

5 The five Fundamental Categories of Personality, Matter, Energy, Space and Time and the essence of their use in the Colon Classification.

This book is not presented in the form of a continuous narrative. The pages are divided into individually numbered frames. On many of these frames you will be asked a question. The answer you give or select will direct you to the next frame you should read.

You begin on frame 203, the first frame of this second volume of the course.

SECTION 1: UNIVERSAL DECIMAL CLASSIFICATION/PART I

In this section of the course you will be introduced to the Universal Decimal Classification which will be referred to throughout as the UDC. This is the scheme you will use for the remainder of your practical classification.

This section is intended to provide you with basic instruction and practice in the use of UDC as an indexing language for the classification of documents at the level of summarisation.

The first edition of UDC was published in 1905. It was initially intended for use in the classified arrangement of a grandiose index to all recorded human knowledge, a 'universal index'. To this end it was developed by two Belgians, Paul Otlet and Henri La Fontaine, using the Decimal Classification of Melvil Dewey as the basis for their new scheme.

The idea of the universal index eventually came to nothing, but the UDC found favour as a general classification scheme and continued to develop in its own right.

The Fédération Internationale de Documentation (FID) is the international body with overall responsibility for the revision and maintenance of UDC. This responsibility is vested in the Central Classification Committee of FID which works in cooperation with the numerous national committees of the member countries.

The first and second editions of UDC, 1905 and 1927-1933 respectively, were both in French. The third edition, commenced in 1934 and completed in 1952, appeared in German. In 1943 work was begun on a fourth edition, to be published in English. At the time of writing (1975) this edition is only just nearing completion.

An abridged version of the full UDC schedules was first published in English in 1948 by the British Standards Institution, the official British editorial body for the scheme.

In this course you will be using the *3rd Abridged English Edition* of UDC. This was first published by the British Standards Institution in 1961 as *BS1000A:1961*. Make very certain that your copy of UDC is the *Abridged English Edition, 3rd Edition, Revised 1961*. All references in this course are made to this latest abridgement.

At this point, before you go on to use UDC, it might be helpful to make some comments regarding this scheme and the Colon Classification (CC). These may help to answer the question, often asked by students, 'Why bother to learn about Colon, if we are going to use UDC?'.

CC and UDC are both *general* classification schemes. They both face the problems presented in attempting to provide a system for the classification of all areas of knowledge.

In CC you have a classification scheme which is based on precisely defined principles, and postulates, and which adheres strictly to these principles (see Volume 1 of this course).

The UDC, in its basic structure, predates CC and, as we shall see, it lacks much of this latter scheme's consistency and predictability.

Ranganathan's research into classification theory and practice, much of which is incorporated in his Colon Classification, is of accepted basic value in modern classification. It is therefore justifiable, and helpful, to view UDC in terms of Ranganathan's analysis of the problems of classification.

It is, however, essential to keep the historical context of UDC firmly in mind when studying and using the scheme. The results of more recent research may well elucidate parts of the scheme and improve its use in practical classification, but, ultimately, it must be seen as an indexing language in its own right to be used within its own limitations.

Now turn to your copy of the Abridged English Edition of UDC (BS1000A:1961).

As a prelude to using the scheme, we will briefly outline the various sections of this book. You will find a contents list on page 2 of your copy.

Introductory material pp 3-9. On these pages you will find descriptive and explanatory notes regarding the scheme. It would be wise to delay reading these until you have had some experience in using the scheme.

Tables of auxiliaries pp 10-25. These are auxiliary schedules, available for use in classification in conjunction with the main schedules. You will be referred to them when appropriate.

Main tables pp 27-145. These constitute the main schedules of the classification scheme. Do not forget that the schedules you have in front of you are an *abridged* version of the full UDC schedules. A list of some of the other editions of UDC can be found at the end of the book on page 254.

Alphabetical index pp 147-253. This is the alphabetical index to the schedules of the classification.

First of all we will consider the main schedules or *'main tables'*, so turn to page 26 of the scheme where you will find an outline of the main divisions of these schedules.
Continue on the next frame

UDC divides the whole of knowledge initially into ten broad areas. Each of these ten divisions is allocated a notation of one digit, thus:

0 Generalities
1 Philosophy
2 Religion
3 Social sciences
4 Linguistics
5 Natural sciences
6 Applied sciences
7 The Arts
8 Literature
9 History and Geography

You will see these divisions, with their notations, printed in bold type on page 26. The notation for Generalities, 0, is omitted.

It is interesting to note that these ten divisions bear a certain correlation, admittedly only a broad one, with the idea of Fundamental Disciplines, mentioned earlier in this course. With the exceptions of 0 Generalities, which in this scheme does *not* represent a unified discipline, and 4, Linguistics, which we would not regard as a Fundamental Discipline, the other primary divisions show this broad correlation.

Each of the ten primary divisions is successively subdivided into more narrowly defined subject fields.

The outline on page 26 of the scheme presents the major subdivisions. Thus, within 3, Social sciences, you find such subdivisions as,

32 Political science
37 Education

Within 5, Natural sciences, there are

51 Mathematics
52 Astronomy
53 Physics

and so on.

We shall examine the further, and more detailed, divisions presented in the main tables in due course. First cast your mind back to our examination of CC (Volume 1 of this course).

You will recall that the primary divisions of knowledge within CC are referred to as the main classes of that scheme.

Each main class in CC is a traditionally recognised discipline, or area of study, such as Agriculture (class J) or Geography (class U).

In UDC, it is usual to call the *first ten divisions*, 0 Generalities, 1 Philosophy, 2 Religion, etc, the *main classes* of the scheme.

The sub-divisions of these ten main classes, eg

02   Librarianship
32   Political science
61   Medical science

are *sub-classes* within the scheme.

You will see that many of these sub-classes, the ones just mentioned, for example, correspond to *main classes* in CC.

This is because the concept of a 'main class' is usually defined in the literature of classification in terms of the notational plane. That is, the main classes of a scheme are the primary divisions of that scheme *as expressed in its notation*.

If a classification scheme employed, say, capital letters, A, B, C, D, etc, as the notation for its main classes, it could provide conveniently for twenty-six main classes.

UDC is based on Melvil Dewey's Decimal Classification. The Decimal Classification uses arabic numerals, divided decimally, for its notation. This notation provides conveniently for *ten* main classes, 000, 100, 200, etc, to 900.

This basic structure of ten main classes is retained by UDC, although Dewey's three digit base for each main class is dropped.

Which of the following statements is true?

Each classification scheme defines its main classes in accordance with the Fundamental Disciplines.	– frame 209
Each classification scheme defines its own set of main classes.	– frame 213

---

205   (215)

Your answer 03(091).

No, you are repeating the same kind of mistake. You are still failing to distinguish between terms representing form concepts and the same terms representing subject concepts.

Please return to frame 211. Read through the text carefully and attempt the question again.

206 (219)

Your answer, 61 "17". Yes, this is the correct class number for the document *'Eighteenth century medicine'*.

Dates are expressed in UDC as numerical statements. Centuries are denoted by their *first two* digits only. The concept 'eighteenth century' or *'the 1700s'* is thus expressed as "17".

Space, or as UDC prefers, *Place*, concepts are listed in schedule (e) on pages 12-21. Turn now to this schedule.

The notations for Space concepts are enclosed in round brackets, ( ), and added to the main table numbers when required for the further subdivision of a class.

Political and *administrative* areas are enumerated for you in schedule (e)

    eg   (420)   England

            (423.8) Somerset

Physiographic divisions of the earth's surface are also enumerated

    eg   (22) Islands

            (23) Mountains

In addition, UDC provides for certain Space concepts such as *orientation*. These concepts are always used in conjunction with some other Space division, political or physiographic, and are introduced by - (hyphen).

    eg   'Coal mining in Somerset'   622.333(423.8)

           'Coal mining in north Somerset' 622.333(423.8-17)

Select the correct class number for a document about *'The folklore of the West Riding of Yorkshire'*.

    398(427.4-15)   – frame 227

    39 (427.4-15)   – frame 216

    398(427.415)   – frame 243

---

207 (228)

Your answer 663.93.047. Good. This is quite correct.

In order to denote the concept 'freeze-drying' you have used one of the special auxiliaries enumerated under 66.0.

Freeze-drying is denoted by the special auxiliary .047. It is introduced in a class mark by the facet indicator .0 (point nought).

Now please turn to frame 221 where you will find another example of the use of special auxiliaries.

208 (214)

You say that the correct class number is 611.2. You are wrong.

If you consult the alphabetical index under 'Respiratory system', 611.2 is one of the class numbers to which you are referred.

However, on checking the schedules, you can see that 611.2 is a subdivision of class *611 Anatomy*. It represents the *anatomy* of the respiratory system. The concept *disease* is *not* provided for in this class number.

Return to frame 214, select another answer to the question and this time check the context of the class number in the schedules carefully.

---

209 (204)

(NB: Numbers given in brackets refer to frames which have led to the one you are reading. This is to help you retrace your steps if necessary.)

You say that each classification scheme defines its main classes in accordance with the Fundamental Disciplines. No, this is not true.

We did say that the main classes in UDC bear a broad correlation with the Fundamental Disciplines—Philosophy, Religion, Natural science, etc.

But what about CC? Agriculture, Education, Economics, Political science are all *main classes* within this scheme but they are not Fundamental Disciplines.

Please return to frame 204 and read through what was said about main classes again. Then select the correct answer to the question and proceed with the course.

210 (214)

Your answer 616.2. Correct.

616.2 is a subdivision of class *616 Disease* and it specifies *respiratory diseases.*

In some cases, then, as in *'Diseases of the respiratory system'*, UDC provides the indexer with a ready-made class number for a compound subject.

This scheme does *enumerate* some compound subjects. In the above example you were able to find an enumerated class number in the main tables which provided an adequate translation of your subject analysis. No synthesis was required.

Unlike CC, UDC does not confine its enumeration to isolate concepts.

The enumeration of compound subjects is, however, limited. UDC recognises, to a high degree, the value of *synthesis* in classification. In the great majority of cases you will employ some synthesis when classifying documents by this scheme.

There are many provisions within the scheme which allow for the synthesis of concepts in the notational expression of compound subjects.

We shall look first at the *COMMON AUXILIARIES*. These are located under the *Tables of auxiliaries* beginning on page 10. So turn now to this part of the scheme.

Continue on the next frame

The *COMMON AUXILIARIES* are so called because their schedules are *auxiliary* to the main tables and *common* in that they are available for the sub-division of *all* classes.

You have already used such 'common subdivisions' when providing for Space, Time and Forms concepts in CC.

Let us look first at the common auxiliaries of Form, schedule (d) on page 11 of the scheme.

The majority of this schedule is devoted to various *forms of presentation*,

eg   (048)   Abstracts

       (083)   Formulae

Physical forms are also included,

eg   (086.4) Globes and relief maps

       (086.7) Gramophone records, tapes

We may note that the concept of *intellectual form* is also provided for,

eg   (091)   Historical presentation

The common auxiliaries of Form are identified in a class number by their own distinctive facet indicator (0...).

Remember, they are available for the subdivision of *any* class if required. You do *not* need to receive explicit instructions in the main tables indicating their availability.

Look, for example, at the way in which the class numbers for the following documents are derived by referring to the appropriate parts of the index and classified schedules.

Title: *'A directory of civil engineering'*
SA: Engineering/Civil/Directory
Class no: 624(058.7)

Title: *'A dictionary of psychology'*
SA: Psychology/Dictionary
Class no: 159.9(03)

As we said in the section of this course devoted to subject analysis (Volume 1), it is important to distinguish carefully between terms representing true *form* concepts and the *same* terms representing *subject* concepts.

Take, for example, a document titled *'A history of periodicals'*.

Which of the following is the correct class number for this document?

93(051)   – frame 215

05(091)   – frame 219

212 (215)

Your answer 93(03). Correct.

In this case, *'A dictionary of history'*, 'history' is the subject concept and 'dictionary' the form concept.

You have made the correct distinction in your subject analysis and translated accurately.

Please turn to frame 219 and continue with the course.

(NB: Numbers given in brackets refer to frames which have led to the one you are reading. This is to help you retrace your steps if necessary.)

You say that each classification scheme defines its own set of main classes. Yes, this is quite true.

Main classes are thus only capable of *precise* definition in the contexts of particular classification schemes. That which constitutes a main class according to the notation of one scheme, does not necessarily constitute a main class in another scheme. This can be seen in a comparison of the main classes of CC and UDC.

There is, however, a tendency to employ the term 'main class' in the *idea plane* of practical classification. Thus, in the subject analysis of a document, the *discipline* to which a document belongs is often referred to as its 'main class'.

We have done this when working with CC, for, in that scheme, the discipline concepts recognized in subject analyses usually correspond *directly* to main classes in the schedules.

In our future subject analyses of documents, for the purposes of classification by UDC, we shall use the term *BASIC CLASS* to distinguish disciplines from phenomena studied by disciplines.

We shall reserve the term *main class* to denote structural divisions of particular classification schemes.

UDC, then, has ten main classes

You have seen that these main classes, with the exception of 0 Generalities, represent discipline concepts. In several cases they correspond to Fundamental Disciplines.

At the first level of sub-division of most of the main classes, we find sub-classes which usually represent sub-disciplines.

Look at the schedule of main class *5, Mathematics and Natural sciences,* on page 59 of the scheme. You will see that the first major sub-class is *51 Mathematics.* On page 61 you will find class *52 Astronomy* followed by *53 Physics and Mechanics.*

Now carry on through the schedule for main class 5 and note the major sub-classes into which it is divided. Their headings are printed in bold type across the centre of the pages. You will see that each of these sub-classes constitutes a sub-discipline Geology, Botany, etc.

The basic principle of UDC, as with CC, and all the major general classification schemes, is to classify documents *first* according to the disciplines to which they belong.

A word of warning is advisable at this early stage, however. There are very few principles in UDC which are applied *strictly* throughout the scheme. In this sense the scheme differs widely from CC.

UDC is essentially a pragmatic scheme and, in many instances, pragmatic decisions override classificatory principles. As you will see, this makes for a lack of consistency.

In many areas, the scheme allows a great deal of freedom to the indexer in its usage. This is in contrast to CC, which was the first major scheme to prescribe very precise rules as to its application.

Because of this degree of freedom, the indexer must formulate his own rules when applying UDC. Otherwise the situation would become chaotic.

In your practical classification with UDC you are going to employ as your guide some of the principles which we have already established as useful (Volume 1).

This is particularly so at the very important stage of the subject analysis of documents. As with CC, your subject analyses will be *specific summarisations* of the dominant theme of each document.

You are required to cast these analyses in the citation order PME...ST Form. The reasons for this will become increasingly clear.

To help you arrive at this order, and to help you identify P M and E isolates, you have been provided with the table showing the categories and citation order in CC. The classes have been arranged in UDC order, that is in the order in which they appear in the UDC main tables. Do not forget to refer to this table in your practical classification, frames 349-352.

Continue on the next frame

We will begin to classify by UDC at its level of least complexity. This will serve to introduce you to the alphabetical index to the schedules.

Suppose you have to classify the following document,

Title: *'The psychology of perception'*

SA: Psychology/Perception

Here you have a compound subject consisting of a basic class, psycholog and one isolate, perception.

Consult the alphabetical index under the term perception (page 216). You will see the following entry:

Perception. Cf Intuition; Sensory. . .

occult 133.3

That part of the entry, *occult 133.3,* tells you that the concept perception occurs in the classified schedule at class number 133.3.

Turn to this part of the schedule (page 30). Perception appears here in main class 1, Philosophy in the context of 133 occultism. The subdivision 133.3 gives you, specifically, occult perception. You have decided, in your subject analysis, that this document belongs to the basic class Psychology. You do not wish to use perception in the context of occultism and therefore you reject this class number.

Return to your alphabetical index entry. That part of the entry, *Cf Intuition, sensory. . .,* tells you that you should also consider those entries under the terms *Intuition* and *Sensory* (perception).

Sensory perception appears to fit your particular context so consult this entry. Here you will see

Sensory perception   159.937

animals   591.185

You do not want sensory perception *in animals,* so consult the schedules under 159.937 (page 31).

Here you find perception as a subdivision of class 159.93 Sensation. Sense perception which, in turn, is a subdivision of the class 159.9 Psychology.

You need go no further. Your desired class number, the translation of your subject analysis, is enumerated for you in the schedules, namely,

159.937

Remember, never classify by the alphabetical index alone. Always check the schedules to ensure that the desired concept is in the desired context.

Now take the following document:

    Title: *'Diseases of the respiratory system'*
    SA: Medicine/Respiratory system/Diseases
  Which of the following is the correct class number?
    616   – frame 218
    611.2   – frame 208
    616.2   – frame 210

---

215 (211)

You think that the correct class number is 93(051). No, you are wrong.

The document was titled *'A history of periodicals'.* In this case the term 'periodicals' represents the *subject* of the document. It is *about* periodicals. It is not itself a periodical.

In your class number 'periodicals' appears as a form concept, while 'history', which in this instance represents a concept of intellectual form, appears as the subject of the document.

Now try another example.

Which of the following is the correct class number for the document *'A dictionary of history'?*

    93(03)   – frame 212
    03(091)   – frame 205

216 (206)

You say that the class number is 39(427.4-15). No, this is wrong.

This class number is not *specific* enough for the subject of the document. Return to frame 206, check the index and the schedules for class 39 carefully before selecting another answer to the question.

---

217 (228)

Your answer 663.047. No, this is not correct.

This class number is not specific enough for the subject of the document. You have specified 'beverages' but not the particular beverage in question, coffee.

Please return to frame 228. Check the index and the schedule for class 663 carefully. Then select the correct answer to the question and proceed with the course.

---

218 (214)

Your answer 616. No, this is incorrect.

You might have arrived at this class number by consulting the alphabetical index under the term 'disease'.

616 *does* represent the concept disease, or pathology, in class 61 Medical sciences. But what about 'respiratory system', is this provided for in the class number 616? The answer is no.

Return to frame 214, select another answer to the question and check the class number carefully in the schedules.

219 (211)

Your answer 05(091). Correct.

In this case, '*A history of periodicals*', the term 'periodicals' represents the *subject* of the document. As a subject concept it appears in the Generalities main class at 05. 'History' is the *form* concept, provided for in UDC as common auxiliary (091), historical presentation.

Let us now consider *Time* concepts. These are listed in schedule (g) of the common auxiliaries, page 22. The facet indicator for Time is " " (quotation marks).

Dates are expressed numerically and enclosed in quotation marks. Examples are provided in the notes to schedule (g) which you should read through. Here you will see illustrated the notations for individual days, years, decades and centuries. There is obviously no need to provide an exhaustive enumeration.

Certain aspects of Time which *do* require a specifically allocated notation are enumerated under '*Other time aspects*', eg "313" Future.

Which of the following is the correct class number for the document '*Eighteenth century medicine*'?

61 "18"	– frame 229
61 "1800"	– frame 226
61 "17"	– frame 206

220 (234)
Your answer 351.741.082. Correct.

In order to denote the concept 'promotion' you have used the special auxiliaries enumerated at 35.07/.08. You have this time utilised the correct facet indicator .0 (point nought).

Please go on to frame 221 where you will find another example of the use of special auxiliaries.

---

221 (207, 220)
This time we will try an example taken from the discipline Architecture.

The document is about *'Islamic architecture'*.

Which of the following is the correct class number for this document?

72.7.033.3	– frame 230
7.033.3	– frame 235
72.033.3	– frame 240

222 (241)

Your choice, 911.3:61(5). Yes, this is the correct class number for the document *'A medical geography of Asia'.* In this class number, the concept 'medicine' is taken from its location as class 61 and linked by the colon to 911.3, Human geography. Asia is provided for by the common auxiliary of Place, (5).

In class 911 you are *instructed* to divide by the rest of the classification, when required, using the colon.

You need not, however, receive these explicit instructions before you proceed to use this device. You are free to sub-divide *any* class in UDC by any other appropriate part of the schedules in this manner, if this should be required.

If a concept is neither directly enumerated as part of a compound, nor provided as a special auxiliary of the class in which you are working, nor as a common auxiliary, it can be taken from any relevant part of the schedules in which it does occur.

We stress *relevant*. When 'borrowing' such a concept always check its precise context in the schedules to ensure that it is appropriate to your needs. Moreover, the *full* class number must always be used to ensure that this precise context is expressed.

Which of the following is the correct class number for the document *'The circulation of sap in cactuses'?*

> 582.85:631.577 — frame 232
> 582.85:581.112 — frame 245
> 582.85:1.112   — frame 242

223 (246)

You think that this represents a *compound* subject. No, you are wrong.

Earlier in this course (Volume 1) we defined a compound subject as consisting, at the level of summarisation, of *a basic subject and two or more of its isolates*.

The analysis of this document in question reveals another kind of element.

Please return to frame 246 and read through the explanation of phase relations again. Then consider the question once more and select the correct answer.

---

224 (244)

Your answer 546.13/546.14. No, you are not right in this.

You have attempted to aggregate the UDC class number incorrectly.

Please return to frame 244 and read again about the use of the / (oblique stroke), paying particular attention to the examples given. Then check the schedules carefully when selecting the correct answer to the question.

---

225 (244)

Your answer 546.13. This is incorrect.

The document in question is about *'The chemistry of chlorine and bromine'*.

Your class number donotes *'The chemistry of chlorine'*.

Return to frame 244 and read again about the aggregation of class numbers. Then select another answer to the question and proceed with the course.

226 (219)

Your answer 61 "1800". No, this is incorrect.

Dates are expressed *numerically* in UDC. You simply take the numerical statement of, say, a particular year and enclose this in " " (quotation marks). In other words you have a ready-made notation, eg

  1066 AD "1066"
  1972 AD "1972"

If you wish to denote a century, you use the first *two digits* of that century's *numerical statement,* eg

  Twentieth century "19"

Your class number denotes 'Medicine in the year *1800', not* 'Eighteenth century medicine'.

Please return to frame 219 and select the correct answer to the question.

---

227 (206)

Your answer 398(427.4-15). Right.

Yorkshire is specified as (427.4). If we wish to denote the *West Riding* of Yorkshire we use the notation (-15) for the concept *'west',* hence (427.4-15).

We shall mention some of the other common auxiliaries of UDC in due course.

Remember that, like Space, Time and Form, *common auxiliaires* are available for the subdivision of *any* class when required.

You can, of course, use *more than one* common auxiliary if this is necessary in the specification of a subject.

  Eg *'An encyclopedia of the folklore of the West Riding of Yorkshire'*
    398(427.4-15)(03)

Continue on the next frame

So far you have seen two ways in which UDC provides for the classification of concepts.

    1 Direct enumeration of compound subjects in the main tables

    2 Provision of common auxiliaries

We are now going to look at a third method, the use of *SPECIAL AUXILIARIES.*

It was said earlier that the enumeration of compound subjects in UDC is restricted. The scheme employs the principle of synthesis to a high degree. The common auxiliaries allow for some synthesis but they are obviously insufficient by themselves. The special auxiliaries allow the process of synthesis to be taken one stage further.

In many of its classes, UDC lists certain concepts once only as *'special auxiliaries'* of that class. These special auxiliaries are available for the further sub-division of that class when required.

You are already familiar with the idea of enumerating isolate concepts in the rigorous facet analysis of CC. The special auxiliaries of UDC represent a less systematically developed use of facet analysis.

Special auxiliaries are identified by the facet indicators,

    - (hyphen)

and

    .0 (point nought)

There is also a restricted use of special auxiliaries introduced by ' (apostrophe) in parts of the Chemistry class which we need not pursue in this course. (See section (k) on page 25 of the scheme for explanatory notes on special auxiliaries.)

Special auxiliaries are listed in the main tables and are 'special' in the sense that their use is restricted to those classes of which they form an integral part.

You do not always receive explicit instructions on the schedules as to the exact extent of the applicability of these auxiliaries. In many cases this has to be inferred from the position in any given class.

Look, for example, at *class 3, Social sciences,* on page 36. Here you will see that the concepts in the *Persons* facet of class 3 are provided for by special auxiliaries enumerated at 3-05.

These auxiliaries can be applied *throughout* class 3 if required. They are *not* repeated in each of its sub-classes

    Eg   *'Sociology of young people'*

            Sociology/Young people

            301-053.7

Now turn to *class 66 Chemical industry. Chemical technology,* on page 116.

Initially you receive the instruction

   66-2/-8 As 621-2/-8 plant, processes, product details.

This tells you that you may use the special auxiliaries already enumerated at 621-2/-8, and therefore not repeated here in full.

   Eg *'Safety installations in the manufacture of high explosives'*
      Technology/Chemical industry/High explosives/Safety installations
      662.2-781

At 66.0 you are provided with another set of special auxiliaries. These represent *Operations* and *Processes.* These are also available for use throughout class 66 and are enumerated at this point in the schedules.

   Now consider a document about *'The freeze drying of coffee'.* We could summarise this as

      Technology/Drinks industry/Coffee/Freeze drying

   Which of the following is the correct class number for this document?

      663.93-047   – frame 234
      663.047   – frame 217
      663.93.047   – frame 207

---

229 (219)

Your answer 61 "18". No, this is incorrect.

   We said that *dates* are expressed *numerically.* Centuries are denoted by the *first two* digits of their numerical statement.

   "18" thus indicates the 1800s, or the *nineteenth century.*

   Please return to frame 219 and select another answer to the question.

230 (221)

You say that the correct class number is 72.7.033.3. No, you are wrong.

The special auxiliaries to which you have recourse in this case are enumerated under 7.0.

These are available for use in class 72 Architecture, but you are *not* required to repeat the *entire* notation, eg 7.033.3, when subdividing class 72 by one of these special auxiliaries.

Please return to frame 221 and select the correct answer. Check its method of construction carefully in the schedules.

---

231 (241)

You say 911:61(5). No, this is wrong.

You have specified the concepts 'medical' and 'Asia' correctly. Class 911 is, however, subdivided into physical geography and human geography *before* the use of the colon is resorted to.

You have not observed these prior divisions in your class number but have 'coloned' directly to 911.

Please return to frame 241. Select the correct class number and check its construction carefully in the schedules.

232 (222)
You say 582.85:631.577. No, you are wrong.

On consulting the index under the term 'sap' you are referred to 631.577. However, it was said that you must always check the precise context of a concept *in the schedules* to ensure that it is appropriate to your needs.

Please return to frame 222 and select another answer to the question while remembering to observe this rule.

---

233 (246)
You think this represents a *simple* subject. You are wrong.

Earlier in this course (Volume 1) we defined a simple subject as consisting, at the level of summarisation, of *a basic subject and one isolate drawn from that area of knowledge*, eg Religion/Christianity.

The analysis of the document in question certainly produces more elements than these.

Please return to frame 246 and read through the explanation of phase relations again. Then consider the question once more and select the correct answer.

234 (228)

Your answer 663.93-047. No, you are wrong.

We said that there are two facet indicators for the special auxiliaries

- (hyphen)

and

.0 (point nought)

The facet indicator to be used for any particular special auxiliary is dictated in the schedules where that auxiliary is enumerated.

In this instance you are using the special auxiliaries enumerated at *66.0*. These auxiliaries are therefore introduced by .0 (point nought) *not* - (hyphen).

Now try another example.

The document is titled *'Promotion of personnel in the police force'*. This is summarised as

Public administration/Public services/Police/Promotion

Which of the following is the correct class number?

351.741-082   − frame 239

351.741.082   − frame 220

---

235 (221)

You say that 7.033.3 is the correct class number. No, you are wrong.

This class number fails to denote the discipline concept Architecture. You have simply located the notation for the particular *special auxiliary* that you wish to employ.

Return to frame 221 and select the correct answer to the question.

236 (244)

Your answer 546.13/.14. Quite correct.

You have aggregated the class numbers for the concepts 'chlorine' and 'bromine' to produce the distinct class number 546.13/.14. In constructing this aggregate class number, you have rightly omitted a repetition of the digits 546 following the / (oblique stroke).

The + (plus sign) can be used for adding *non-consecutive* UDC class numbers.

In this way the indexer can link two or more concepts, associated in the literature but separated in the UDC schedule order.

When using the + (plus sign) the *full* class number for each concept is *always* used

      Eg   *'The chemistry of chlorine and fluorine'*
             546.13+546.16

Construct a class number, using the + (plus sign), for the document *'Economic geology and mining in the USA'.* Then turn to frame 248.

---

237 (246)

You say that the document about *'The influence of religion on Renaissance art'* represents a complex subject. Correct.

The summarisation of this document would be

      Art/Renaissance/*Influenced by*/Religion

This reveals a phase relation of the influence kind. As the subject includes a phase relation it is a *complex subject.*

In UDC we must rely on the : (colon) to indicate a phase relation. We cannot express the particular *kind* of phase relation existing.

The class number for this document is, consequently,

      7.034:2

Continue on the next frame

238 (237)

In certain classes UDC *instructs* the indexer to express a desired concept by a simple *VERBAL* statement.

Look, for example, at *class 8, Literature.* There is no author facet enumerated in this class. Individual authors are not allocated numerical notations.

If you wish to specify an individual author, you do so by simply writing his or her *name*, as instructed

| Eg | *'The works of Charles Dickens'* | 820 DICKENS |
| | *'The poems of Lord Byron'* | 820.1 BYRON |

You do not, however, need to receive instructions in the schedules before you may employ these *VERBAL EXTENSIONS* to UDC class numbers.

In any class, if a desired concept is not specified in the 'normal' UDC notation, it can be individualised by a verbal extension to the class number.

Verbal extensions are particularly useful when specifying individual persons, places, plants, animals, etc, which are not specified in named UDC notation.

Now consider the following document.

Title *'A West Country village: Ashworthy: family, kinship and land'*

This can be summarised as:

Social geography/England/West Country/Village communities/ Ashworthy

Construct a class number for this document using an appropriate verbal extension and then turn to frame 244.

---

239 (234)

Your answer 351.741-082. No, you are wrong.

You are still making the same mistake in that you are failing to use the correct facet indicator for the special auxiliary in question.

Return to frame 234. Read through the text and then select the correct answer to the question remembering to consult the schedules very carefully.

Your answer 72.033.3. Correct.

In class 72, Architecture, the *Style*, or *Period*, facet is provided for by special auxiliaries enumerated at 7.03 and applicable throughout main class 7.

Thus the class number for a document about 'Islamic architecture' is 72.033.3 in which .033.3 is the special auxiliary denoting 'Islamic style'.

As in most other aspects of UDC, there is no hard and fast rule which can be relied upon to predict the occurence of special auxiliaries. Analysis within the scheme is too inconsistent to allow for this.

Each class must be taken as a discrete case. In some the use of special auxiliaries is highly developed; in others non-existent.

Thus, when classifying a document, if a desired concept is not enumerated as part of a compound class number, look to see if it is provided for as a special auxiliary of the class in which you are working.

Continue on the next frame

241 (240)

We now come to the most powerful device for synthesis provided in UDC, the use of the relational sign : (colon).

By means of this device, any class in UDC can be subdivided by any other appropriate part of the scheme, should this be required in the expression of a compound subject. The notations for the concepts thus compounded are linked by the : (colon).

Look, for example, at class 911, General geography, on page 143 of the scheme.

General, or 'systematic', geography is a very wide-ranging area of study encompassing such diverse fields as geomorphology, economic geography, biogeography, etc.

The concepts which define the particular *kind* of systematic geography, economic, cultural, etc, can be regarded as the personality concepts of this class (see CC).

Now in UDC these concepts are not provided for as special auxiliaries of class 911. They do *not* fall within the province of the common auxiliaries nor are they *all* directly enumerated in class 911 as compound subjects. The class is broadly subdivided into Physical geography, 911.2 and Human geography 911.3, which are thus provided for as directly enumerated compounds, but this enumeration does not go into sufficient detail.

Consequently, when one of these concepts is required in the further subdivision of class 911, it is 'borrowed' from another part of the main tables. It is taken from the appropriate class in which it *is* enumerated and linked by a colon to class 911.

You are, in fact, instructed to do this, and provided with examples, in the schedule for class 911, thus,

911.3   Human (cultural) geography. By :3..., :6..., etc.

:32 Political geography   :33 Economic geography

The class number for *Political geography* is, then, *911.3:32,* in which the concept 'political' is taken from its location at class 32, Political science, and joined by the : (colon) to 911.3, Human geography.

According to the same principle, the class number for *Economic geography* is 911.3:33.

The use of the : (colon) in class 911 is a clear illustration of the principle of making the *whole of the classification scheme* available for the sub-division of any given class when required.

This principle is not unique to UDC. Both CC and the Dewey Decimal Classification employ it. In these schemes, however, the device is *only* used to specify the *species of a genus,* eg a particular *kind* of library such as medical or agricultural library.

Its use in UDC is far more widespread. It is the most important provision for synthesis within the scheme and has therefore to be relied upon in many situations. Its usage is less well defined than in either CC or Dewey and is certainly not restricted to the specification of the species of a genus.

Now consider the following document,

'*A medical geography of Asia*'

Which of the following is the correct class number for this document?

911:61(5)   — frame 231

911.3:61:(5)   — frame 247

911.3:61(5)   — frame 222

---

242 (222)

Your answer 582.85:1.112. No, this is wrong.

You must always use the *full* class number for any concept by which you are subdividing a class through the use of the : (colon).

If you do not observe this rule, the resulting class number will be either meaningless or, at least, have the wrong meaning.

Look at your class number again and you will see that it is meaningless. For what concept does the notation: 1.112 stand?

Return to frame 222 and select the correct answer to the question.

---

243 (206)

You say that the class number is 398(427.415). No, you are wrong.

You have incorrectly constructed that part of the class number which specifies the space concept 'West Riding of Yorkshire'.

Return to frame 206 and read what was said about Space concepts again. Then select the correct answer to the question and proceed with the course.

244 (238)
Your class number should be 308(423-202 Ashworthy) *or* 911.3:308(423-202 Ashworthy).

In the above example, when specifying the individual village, Ashworthy we must employ a *verbal extension* to the 'normal' UDC notation.

All the devices which you have so far encountered—common auxiliaries, special auxiliaries, use of the : (colon), verbal extensions—allow for the further *subdivision* of classes.

They thus allow for the *narrowing* of a given class.

UDC also allows the indexer to *widen* or *expand* the scope of a class. This is achieved through the use of two notational devices.

/ (oblique stroke)
+ (plus sign)

We shall consider first the / (oblique stroke). This is used for the linking of *consecutive* UDC class numbers. The result of this is to provide a distinct class number for an aggregate of subjects which are adjacent in the UDC schedule order.

Eg   5/6   Science and technology
      343/347 Criminal and civil law

Thus a document about *'Science and technology in the USSR in 1970'* would receive the class number 5/6 (47) "1970".

If the class numbers for the concepts so aggregated possess *the first three digits* in common, there is no need to repeat these digits following the / (oblique stroke).

Eg   Title   *'The importance of butter and cheese production in the agriculture of Southwest Ireland'*

      SA   Agriculture/Dairy produce/Butter and cheese/SW Irela
      Class no 637.2/.3(417-14)

Now consider the following document, *'The chemistry of chlorine and bromine'.*

Which of the following is the correct class number?

      546.13/546.14   – frame 224
      546.13   – frame 225
      546.13/.14   – frame 236

245 (222)

Your answer 582.85:581.112. Good, this is quite correct.

Remember always to check the precise context of a concept 'borrowed' from another part of the main tables and used for the subdivision of a given class. This is to ensure that the context is appropriate to your needs.

Never classify by the index alone.

Remember always to express this context *in full* by adding the *full class number.*

If these procedures are not carefully observed, the resulting class number can be either meaningless, or, at least, not have the desired meaning.

It might be useful at this point to briefly review the procedures mentioned so far in the classification of documents by UDC.

SUMMARY

1 The subject of the document, as expressed in your subject analysis, may be directly enumerated in the main tables.

2 If this is not the case, the further concepts you wish to express may be provided for by a variety of ways involving synthesis in the notational plane. These are:

3 By means of a special auxiliary, or auxiliaries, applicable only as indicated in the schedules.

4 By means of a common auxiliary, applicable to all classes.

5 By means of the : (colon) which allows you to further divide the class in which you are working by any other relevant part, or parts, of the main tables.

Continue on the next frame

The concepts introduced by the : (colon) may be manifestations of either Personality, Matter or Energy facets within a given compound. Space and Time have their own distinctive facet indicators like all the common auxiliaries.

UDC calls the colon a 'relation' sign and indeed it is. It tells us that a relationship exists between concepts in a compound subject. It does *not* tell us what *kind* of relationship this is. In CC, you will recall, *each* facet has its own distinctive facet indicator. In UDC the colon has to act as an 'all purpose' facet indicator to a very large extent.

This is also true of the facet indicators used to introduce the special auxiliaries, - (hyphen) and .0 (point nought). These notational symbols serve to introduce a special auxiliary, but they do not tell us precisely what *kind* of concept is represented by the auxiliary.

In UDC, the colon is also used to express another important set of relationships which exist between concepts and of which no mention has been made so far. These are called *PHASE RELATIONS*.

Again we owe this term to Ranganathan who recognises five kinds of phase relation. These are:

1 *General phase*
A relationship of a general, or unspecified, nature existing between subjects.

       Eg   Title *'The relationship between geography and history'*
               SA   Geography/*General relation*/History

2 *Bias phase*
Here the subject of a document is directed, or biased, towards a particular group of users.

       Eg   Title *'Statistics for historians'*
               SA   Statistics/*Bias*/Historians

3 *Comparison phase*
Subjects treated on a comparative basis.

       Eg   Title *'The Decimal Classification and the Colon Classification compared'*
               SA   Library science/Classification/Systems/DC/*Compared to*/CC

4 *Difference phase*
The difference between subjects is concentrated upon.

       Eg   Title *'The differences between classical and gothic architecture*
               SA   Architecture/Styles/Classical/*Difference phase*/Gothic

5 *Influencing phase*
The influence of one subject upon another.

    Eg   Title   *'The influence of science on religion'*
          SA   Religion/*Influenced by*/Science

    When the summarised subject of a document includes a phase relation it is usually called a *COMPLEX SUBJECT*. As such it is distinguished from *compound* and *simple* subjects to which reference has been made (Vol 1).
    In CC, each of the five kinds of phase relation is allocated its own individual notation.
    In UDC we have to rely on the : (colon) to indicate the existence of a phase relationship between concepts. We cannot express the precise kind of phase relation existing.
    Consider a document about *'The influence of religion on Renaissance art'*. What kind of subject does this represent?

    Simple   – frame 233
    Compound – frame 223
    Complex   – frame 237

---

247 (241)
Your answer 911.3:61:(5). No, this is incorrect.
    The concept *'Asia'* is provided for by a *common auxiliary* of Place. You are familiar with the use of these common auxiliaries. They are already provided with their individualising facet indicators and there is no need to use the : (colon) when employing them in the further subdivision of a class.
    Please return to frame 241 and select another answer to the question.

Your answer should be 553+622(73).

It must be stated that an extensive use of the + (plus sign) is *neither recommended nor required.*

In the majority of instances where it *could* be employed in the construction of a class number, the documents concerned should be treated as *composite documents* (see Volume 1). That is, they should be regarded as dealing with *two or more discrete subjects* and should be provided with two or more *discrete class numbers.*

In this way, the document about *'Economic geology and mining in the USA'* would be allocated *two* class numbers

   553(73)
   622(73)

However, the occurance of *'and'* in a title usually implies a *relationship* between concepts. For example, *'Science and history'* implies a document about the *relationship* between science and history, not that these are treated as two *separate* subjects.

Thus, in most cases, *neither* the + (plus sign) *nor* two class numbers are required, but rather the use of the : (colon) which indicates a relationship between the concepts so linked.

Now please continue with Part II of this section of the course dealing with UDC on frame 249.

SECTION 1: UNIVERSAL DECIMAL CLASSIFICATION/PART II

In our examination of UDC so far we have made no explicit mention of the problem of citation order in compound subjects. In this part of the course we shall pay particular attention to this problem and consider the extent to which general principles of helpful citation order may be applied to UDC.

You have already seen that practical classification with UDC involves a high degree of synthesis. The indexer is required to analyse the subject of a document into its constituent elements and then to recombine, or synthesise, these concepts within the provisions and limitations of the classification scheme.

In the Colon Classification, the process of synthesis in the construction of compound class numbers is placed under strict control. In all main classes, synthesis is determined by the prescribed citation order PME...ST.

Now the situation in UDC is very different. In general, UDC has *no prescribed citation order*.

It follows from this that the indexer is given a very large degree of choice in deciding upon the citation order of concepts in compound subjects.

We say a degree of choice because the indexer is not given *total* freedom regarding citation order. In certain cases the citation order in compound subjects is predetermined.

Obviously, when a compound subject is *enumerated* in the main tables, ie provided with a *ready-made* class number, then the indexer has no choice in determining the citation order within that compound.

Suppose, for example, that you have to classify a document about *'Diseases of the throat'*.

The subject of this document is provided with a *ready made* class number at *616.22*.

This class number can be analysed as follows:

61	Medicine
616	Disease
616.2	Respiratory disease
616.22	Throat

It can be seen that, in this case, *Part of body* is subordinated to *Disease* and thus the citation order in the compound is:

Medicine/Disease/Respiratory disease/Throat

Because this class number is enumerated, no synthesis, or 'number-building', is required on the part of the indexer. Consequently, the citation order in this compound subject is *predetermined*.

Continue on the next frame

250 (249)

When synthesis is required in the expression of compound subjects, UDC occasionally provides an *indication* of a possible citation order to be followed.

Such an indication is provided by a *directive* in the schedules.

Please turn to class 59 Zoology.

At 591.2 you will see an example of such a directive thus:

591.2 Diseases, injuries, malformations etc.
Zoopathology. Teratology
:592/59 Specific animals affected

We can infer from this directive that UDC expects the citation order in class 59 to be,

Zoology/Disease/Specific animal

Following this directive, a document about 'Diseases of the honey-bee' would be assigned the class number

591.2:595.799

The citation order in this compound class number is

Zoology/Disease/Honey-bee

(NB: We have omitted any reference to the position of the concept 'specific diseases' in the citation order as this raises a problem not to be dealt with here.)

Such directives, however, do *not* have the status of mandatory instructions. UDC certainly does not forbid other possible citation orders, eg, in this case

Zoology/Honey-bee/Disease
595.799:591.2

Consider the document *'A bibliography of physical anthropology'* and its classification by UDC. Which of the following statements is true?

You must assign to this document the class
number 016:572   — frame 266
You may assign to this document the class
number 572:016   — frame 258

Your answer 582.734(Roses):581.24. Yes, you are correct.

As shown in your table, the categories present in the discipline Botany, cited in PME...ST order, are:

$$P_1 \qquad P_2 \qquad E$$

Botany/Plant/Organ/Processes

If we cite the concepts present in a summarisation of the document about *'Fungus diseases of roses'* in this order we get,

$$P_1 \qquad\qquad E$$

Botany/Roses/Fungus diseases

This translates into the UDC class number

582.734(Roses):581.24

Note that in this class number it is necessary to employ a *verbal extensio* in order to specify the concept 'rose'. The class number 582.734 alone is not specific enough as several plants, including roses, must be classed here.

Continue on frame 261

252 (259)
You think that both class numbers are correct. You are right.

The scheme allows for the intercalation of Space concepts and there-fore *both* class numbers are permissable in terms of UDC. In classifying this particular document we can choose *either* of the two citation orders exemplified:

    1 Education/Higher education/Universities/Germany/19th century
               378.4 (430) "18"

    2 Education/Germany,'Higher education/Universities/19th century
               37 (430) 84 "18"

Obviously, once a choice of citation order has been made it must be kept to, otherwise chaos will result.

If, in class 37, the indexer decides to employ citation order 1 above, he must not, at a later date and with another document, use citation order 2.

When a citation order for a given class in a given collection is chosen the alternatives are rejected permanently.

Thus, in any retrieval situation where UDC is the index language used, it is essential for the indexer to determine a citation order formula for each class and to adhere to it in order to maintain consistency.

Continue on the next frame

Although UDC does not *prescribe* a citation order, it does *suggest* a citation order in the introduction to the English Abridged Edition BS1000 A:1961 (page 9, paragraph 5).

The suggested order is stated in terms of:

1 Main table number
2 Special auxiliaries: ' (apostrophe) .0 (point nought) - (hyphen)
3 Common auxiliaries: Viewpoint Place Time Form Language

Now we stress that this is only a *suggested* citation order, you do *not* need to commit it to memory. It is only presented in the introduction as a guide line, not as a rule of the scheme.

This citation order is *broadly* in agreement with one based on categories, such as PME...ST. It does not, however, go far enough in its analysis of concepts.

The surest way to arrive at a helpful and consistent order is to be guided by those *principles* of citation order which have been demonstrated as helpful.

You have already met the citation order PME...ST in the Colon Classification. You are required, for the purposes of this course, to apply this citation order to UDC as far as the scheme will allow.

Continue on the next frame

Ranganathan's five Fundamental Categories of concepts, Personality, Matter, Energy, Space and Time are *recognisable* in UDC and can therefore be used as a guide to selecting a helpful citation order in the construction of compound class numbers.

Moreover, by using the formula PME...ST Form as a general guide to the selection of citation order, consistency in classification will be ensured.

Although these categories of concepts are recognisable in UDC, they are in no way made *explicit* within the scheme. Facet analysis in UDC is, at best, inconsistent. It most certainly does not analyse each subject area into clearly defined facets on the basis of PMEST and display them, accordingly, in the schedule.

However, if you are to use PME...ST as a guide to citation order in your practical classification with UDC, you must be able to identify these categories as they manifest themselves in any given subject area in the scheme.

As an aid to this, you are provided with a table showing the categories, and citation order of these categories, in each of the main classes of the 6th edition of the Colon Classification. Space, Time and Form are omitted from this table as they are common to all the main classes. See frames 349 to 352.

These classes are arranged in UDC order, beginning with 02 Library science and ending with 93 History.

When classifying a document by UDC, consult this table if you are in doubt as to the nature of the categories present, and their precise citation order, in the subject area within which you are working.

Take, for example, a document belonging to the subject area Library science, *'Book selection in school libraries'*.

Consult your table and decide which of the following UDC class numbers for this document conforms to the citation order of concepts PME...ST.

025.21:027.8 — frame 264
027.8:025.21 — frame 260

255 (261)

Your answer: Geography/Manitoba/Economic/Atlases. No, this is not correct.

It is *possible* to employ this citation order in classifying the document *'An economic atlas of Manitoba'* by UDC. The resulting class number is

917.127:33(084.4)

However, the citation order adopted does *not* conform to PME...ST. You have decided to cite the concept 'Manitoba' first. In other words you imply that Manitoba is a Personality concept in Geography and this is not true.

Please return to frame 261 and reconsider the question, consulting your table which gives you the CC analysis of Geography. Then select another answer to the question.

---

256 (259)

Your answer. Only class number B, ie 37(430)84"18", is correct.

No, you are wrong.

Your answer implies that class number A can be regarded as incorrect and this is not true.

Please return to frame 259 and read again about the choice of citation orders in UDC. Then select the correct answer to the question and continue with the course.

257 (261)

Your answer: Geography/Atlases/Manitoba/Economics. No, you are wrong.

You *could* use this citation order when classifying '*An economic atlas of Manitoba*' by UDC. You would arrive at the following class number:

912(084.4)(712.7):33

This citation order does *not*, however, conform to the order PME...ST. The concept cited first is 'atlases' and this does not constitute a Personality concept in Geography.

Please return to frame 261 and reconsider the question. Look at your table which gives you the CC analysis of Geography and then select another answer to the question.

---

258 (250)

Your answer, you may assign the class number 572:016. Correct.

According to the principles of subject analysis, the document '*A bibliography of physical anthropology*' would be summarised as

Physical anthropology/Bibliography

On translating this analysis into UDC, it is found that the scheme provides no common auxiliary of Form for the concept 'bibliography'. In order to denote this concept the indexer must use the main table numbers 011/016.

In this case the appropriate class is 016 Special subject bibliographies. At 016 there is a directive 'By: ...' which tells the indexer to further subdivide this class by appropriate parts of the scheme using the colon. This directive is *not* an instruction and does *not* prevent adherence to the citation order

Physical anthropology/Bibliography

giving the class number   572:016

Continue on the next frame

259 (258)

In the majority of cases, the indexer is granted considerable freedom of choice as to the citation order he adopts in the construction of compound class numbers.

When using the : (colon) to link concepts, the indexer is at liberty to decide in what order the concepts should be cited.

Consider, for example, *'Insect pests: a guide to the pests of houses, gardens, farms and pets'.*

An appropriate UDC class number for this document is,

595.7:591.65

This class number follows the citation order

Zoology/Insects/Economic zoology/Harmful animals

However, UDC equally permits the indexer to assign the class number

591.65:595.7

In this compound class number, the indexer has adopted the citation order

Zoology/Economic zoology/Harmful animals/Insects

In classifying this document, the indexer is free to adopt whichever citation order he considers most helpful. Both the above class numbers are acceptable in terms of UDC.

Another feature of UDC which allows for the flexibility of citation order in the notational plane, is the ability to *intercalate* certain concepts in compound class numbers.

Some of the common auxiliaries are allocated notations in which the facet indicators possess both an *opening* and a *closure* sign. The notations for Place and Time, for example, are

(1/9)

" "

The numerical notations are *enclosed* within ( ), round brackets, and " ", quotation marks.

When concepts possess this kind of 'packaged' notation, it is possible to insert them in any desired position in a compound class number.

This process is referred to as the *intercalation* of concepts. Intercalation increases the degree of freedom in choosing citation order.

Suppose that you have to classify a document about *'The British Liberal Party'.*

This document can be assigned the class number

329.12 (41-4)

Here you have employed the citation order
Politics/Political parties/Liberals/United Kingdom
It can equally be assigned the class number
329 (41-4) 12
In this case you have employed the citation order
Politics/Political parties/United Kingdom/Liberals
This latter citation order, which is the one exemplified in the schedule
at 329, is achieved by *intercalating* the Space concept, United Kingdom,
within the compound class number.

Again, both these class numbers, representing different citation orders,
are equally acceptable by UDC.

Notice that in the class number 329 (41-4) 12 the decimal point has
been dropped. Except when used as a facet indicator in conjunction with
0 (zero), the decimal point in UDC serves only as a separating device employed after three digits. The intercalation of (41-4) after 329 obviates this
function.

Suppose you have to classify a document about *'The development of the
university in Germany during the nineteenth century'*. You consider two
class numbers for this document,

A   378.4 (430) "18"
B   37 (430) 84 "18"

Which of the following statements is true?

Only class number A is correct. — frame 263
Only class number B is correct. — frame 256
Both class numbers are correct. — frame 252

Your answer 027.8:025.21. Correct.

The citation order within the discipline Library science is:

$$P_1 \qquad M \qquad E$$

Library science/Libraries/Stock/Operations

If we cast the summarisation of the document *'Book selection in school libraries'* into the citation order PME...ST, we get, therefore,

$$P_1 \qquad\qquad E$$

Library science/School libraries/Book selection

The translation of this citation order of concepts into UDC notation gives us the class number

　　027.8:025.21

Now try another example, this time from the discipline Botany. Which of the following class numbers for the document *'Fungus diseases of roses'* conforms to the citation order PME...ST?

　　582.734(Roses):581.24　　– frame 251
　　581.24:582.734(Roses)　　– frame 265

As was stated earlier, concepts that can be regarded as manifestations of the categories Personality, Matter, Energy, Space and Time are recognisable in UDC even though these categories are by no means made explicit within the schedules of the scheme.

Consequently, if we are to use PME...ST as a guide in deciding upon a generally helpful citation order in compound subjects, considerable emphasis is placed upon subject analysis.

In practical classification with UDC, thorough and consistent work at the stage of the subject analysis of a document is essential.

At this point, the indexer must decide what categories the constituent concepts of the analysis represent and, therefore, in what order they should *preferably* be cited.

It is to help you make these important decisions that you have been provided with the table showing the CC analysis of subject areas into PM and E categories.

The resulting subject analysis at the level of summarisation will thus state,

1 The subject area to which this document belongs, ie its *basic class*

2 The phenomena studied cast in PME...ST order. Concepts of Form should appear last in the citation order.

The indexer can then translate this analysis into a UDC class number which follows this desired citation order *so far as the limitations of the scheme allow.*

Consider the document *'An economic atlas of Manitoba'*. The following summarisations of this document employ different citation orders.

Which of these subject analyses is cast in the citation order PME...ST Form?

Geography/Manitoba/Economic/Atlases — frame 255
Geography/Economic/Manitoba/Atlases — frame 267
Geography/Atlases/Manitoba/Economics — frame 257

262 (264)

Your decision, 581.24:582.734 (Roses). No, you are repeating the same kind of error.

You are still failing to observe a PME...ST citation order where this is permissable in the construction of a compound class number in UDC.

The class number you chose represents the citation order

Botany/Plant diseases/Fungus diseases/Roses

Look at your table again and you will see that these concepts are *not* cited in the order PME...ST. In the discipline Botany, *Plants* constitute the *Personality* concepts, while *Diseases* fall within the Processes or *Energy* facet.

Please return to frame 264. Consider the question carefully, then select the correct answer and continue with the course.

---

263 (259)

You say that *only* class number A, ie 378.4(430)"18", is correct.

This means that you think class number B is in some way incorrect. This is not true.

Please return to frame 259 and read through the text on the choice of citation order in UDC again. Then select the correct answer and continue with the course.

Your answer 025.21:027.8. No, this is not the correct answer.

This is a perfectly acceptable UDC class number but it does *not* conform to the citation order PME...ST.

Remember that you are asked to follow PME...ST wherever a choice of citation order is given.

Look at your table again and you will see that the citation order in the class Library science is

$$P_1 \qquad M \qquad E$$
Library science/Libraries/Stock/Operations

Consequently, if we cast the subject analysis of the document *'Book selection in school libraries'* in this citation order, we get

$$P_1 \qquad\qquad E$$
Library science/School libraries/Book selection

The translation of this analysis into a UDC class number conforming to the citation order PME...ST gives us, therefore,

027.8:025.21

Now try another example, this time from the discipline Botany. The document is titled *'Fungus diseases of roses'.*

Consult your table showing you the categories present in this discipline, and their citation order, and then decide which of the following UDC class numbers for the above document conforms to the citation order PME...ST.

582.734(Roses):581.24   — frame 251

581.24:582.734(Roses)   — frame 262

265 (260)

Your answer, 581.24:582.734(Roses). No, this time you are wrong.

Although this is an acceptable UDC class number for the document concerned, the citation order it represents does *not* conform to PME...ST.

Remember that you are asked to follow PME...ST wherever a *choice* of citation order is given in UDC.

Please return to frame 260 and consider the question once more. Having consulted your table carefully, select the correct answer and proceed with the course.

---

266 (250)

Your answer, you must assign the class number 016.572. Wrong.

According to the principles of subject analysis, the document '*A bibliography of physical anthropology*' would be summarised as

    Physical anthropology/Bibliography

On translating this analysis into UDC, it is found that the scheme provides no common auxiliary of Form for the concept 'bibliography'. In order that this concept may be denoted the indexer must use the main table numbers 011/016.

In this case the appropriate class is 016 Special subject bibliographies. At 016 there is a directive 'By: . . . ' which tells the indexer to further subdivide this class by appropriate parts of the scheme using the colon eg 016:572.

This directive is *not* an instruction and UDC does *not* prevent adherence to the citation order

    Physical anthropology/Bibliography

giving the class number   572:016.

Please continue with the course on frame 259.

267 (261)

Your answer: Geography/Economic/Manitoba/Atlases. Yes, you are
right.

If we apply the citation order PME...ST Form to the subject area
Geography, we arrive at the above order in the summarisation of this
document.

Economic geography constitutes the Personality concept and this is
followed by Space and Form, thus,

          P   S   Form

Geography/Economic/Manitoba/Atlases

The translation of this analysis, employing the desired citation order,
gives us the class number

     911.3:33(712.7)(084.4)

It should be stated that our use of PME...ST Form is not an attempt
to *force* the Colon Classification upon UDC. We are only employing
this principle of order, which is applicable to all subject areas, as a
guide in deciding upon a helpful citation order in compound subjects
when such a choice is allowed.

It might be helpful to recapitulate briefly upon what has been said
about citation orders in UDC and the way in which you are required to
apply the scheme for the purposes of this course.

You should then attempt some examples of practical classification
for yourself.

SUMMARY

1 UDC has no *prescribed* citation order.
2 In the majority of cases, it is the responsibility of the indexer to decide
upon the citation order to be employed in compound subjects.
3 In such a situation, it is essential to decide upon a citation order
formula for each class *and to adhere strictly to it.*
4 The surest way to arrive at such a decision is to be guided by principles
of helpful citation order.
5 One such principle is the citation order based upon the categories
PMEST. This is applicable to all subject areas.
6 You are required to follow the citation order PME...ST Form *whenever
a choice of citation order is given.*

Continue on the next frame

268   (267)

It would now be useful for you to classify the following examples by UDC before going on to the next section of the course.

For each document produce:

a) a subject analysis, at the level of summarisation, cast in the citation order PME...ST form.

b) a UDC class number which employs this citation order as far as the scheme will allow.

Remember the tables on frames 349 to 352 which may help in your analyses and then check your answers against those suggested on frame 35

1   Library resources in the Greater London area: No 5 Agricultural libraries.

2   Therapy through hypnosis.

3   Cereal diseases: Ministry of Agriculture, Fisheries and Food Bulletin No 129.

4   Roots of contemporary American architecture: a series of essays.

5   The selected poems of Robert Graves.

Continue on frame 353

SECTION 2: SUBJECT CATALOGUING: A FOREWORD

We must now return to the consideration of indexes and here we shall recapitulate, and expand, upon some of the points already made in *Volume 1
Section 1: Introduction to subject indexing.* You may therefore find it
useful to refer back to the introductory section of that volume.

This present brief section is to be read as preliminary to a more detailed
examination of some of the techniques of index construction which will
follow.

You will recall that a *library catalogue* constitutes a complete record
of the library's collection of documents. From now on we shall refer to
them simply as *catalogues.*

Bibliographies are distinguished from catalogues in that the documents
they record are not necessarily held in a particular library. The limitations
placed upon the documents included in a bibliography are those such as
place of publication, date of publication or subject content.

An *index,* in the context of information retrieval, is some kind of
physical mechanism, or tool, which serves to indicate to the searcher
those parts of an information store which are potentially relevant to a
request.

Catalogues and bibliographies are both forms of indexes. They are
similar in function and in structure. For the purposes of our practical
subject indexing we shall concentrate on, and refer principally to, the
construction of catalogues.

In the process of information retrieval catalogues help to overcome
the limitations of the shelf arrangement of documents, itself a form of
index. They do this primarily by providing *multiple access* to documents
via the medium of document *substitutes* or *representations.*

Catalogues are found in a variety of *physical forms,* for example,
printed book catalogues, sheaf catalogues and *card catalogues.* You can
find descriptions of these types of catalogue in other textbooks and we
need not pursue them in any detail here.

The essential functions of a catalogue, and the principles upon which it
is constructed, are not affected by its physical form. In this course we
are concerned with the *principles* of catalogue construction and therefore
physical form is of little direct interest. Nevertheless, it is important to
envisage the appearance of a catalogue and for this reason we shall refer,
almost exclusively, to the widely adopted card catalogue in our consideration of catalogue construction.

(NB: The method of indexing called *post-coordinate indexing* gives rise to physical forms of indexes which differ from the more 'traditional' catalogues mentioned above. These, and the principles upon which they are constructed, are not to be considered in this volume.)

In a card catalogue, each document substitute is in the form of an *index card* or *catalogue card* usually of a standard size 5 x 3 inches.

We have already seen, (Volume 1), that theoretically a document can have any number of such substitutes or representations in the catalogue. Each document substitute constitutes an *entry* in the catalogue for that document. Practical considerations do, in fact, limit the number of entries that it is feasible to make for any given document.

Now each entry indicates the inclusion of the document within a particular class of documents. These classes are defined by such characteristics *authorship* or *subject content.*

Since it is possible to have a number of entries for a single document we are able to display that document in a number of classes to which it belongs. Thus we provide for *multiple access* to the document. That is access via the different characteristics which it possesses and which might be helpful for the purposes of its retrieval.

Each entry made for a document contains a statement of a class of which the document forms a part. These statements form the *heading* of the entry (written at the top or 'head' of say a catalogue card) and entries are arranged or filed according to their headings which may be either verbal or notational statements.

Those entries which show the inclusion of documents in classes defined by authorship are called *author entries,* in classes defined by subject content, *subject entries.*

If an entry acts as a substitute or representation of a document it must contain a *description* of that document in order to individualise it. These document descriptions include such elements as the document's author, its title, publisher, place and date of publication, pagination, etc.

In order that we can retrieve the document itself, each entry must also state *precisely* where in the library that document is stored or shelved. This locational element is sometimes referred to as the *call mark* or *call number* of the document.

The call number of a document is *not* synonymous with its *class number.* When a library arranges its documents in classified order, the class number of a document is obviously an important element in its call number. The call number may well include other elements, however, such as a *collection number* indicating the particular collection in which the document is housed, eg reference collection.

Not *all* library collections are arranged in classified order. In these cases a document will possess no class number but it must still be provided with a call number for locational purposes. Sometimes accession order is used as an alternative to classified order in the shelf arrangement of documents. In such a situation the accession number of a document will act as its call number and indicate its precise shelf location.

So far we have established that the library catalogue, as an index to the library's collection, contains entries which play the role of document substitutes displaying the inclusion of documents in classes defined by different characteristics. These classes are stated in the headings on the document entries. In response to requests for information we search those classes of documents, ie limited parts of the total store, which are *potentially relevant* to the request. Having located a potentially relevant class, the catalogue will reveal the individual documents contained in that class and will tell the searcher just where these documents can be found within the library.

In addition to entries for individual documents, catalogues also contain directions which *refer* the searcher from one heading to another heading under which potentially relevant information, in the form of document entries, can be located. These are called *references* in the catalogue and thus we have *author references, title references, subject references,* etc, depending on the type of heading referred to and from.

The assigning of author and title headings for entries and references in catalogues is commonly termed *author/title cataloguing* or *author/title indexing.*

It is not the particular concern of this course.

Sets of rules have been formulated to guide the cataloguer in author/ title cataloguing and to help ensure standardisation of practice. Such a *code of cataloguing rules* is the *Anglo-American cataloguing rules* published in 1967, (AACR 1967).

The *description* of documents in catalogue entries is called *descriptive cataloguing* and this also falls outside our present interest. Again, rules have been formulated to ensure standardisation of practice in descriptive cataloguing and these are contained in such codes as AACR 1967.

This course is devoted to *practical subject indexing* and thus our prime concern is with the construction of headings and references which facilitate the retrieval of documents, through the medium of indexes, in response to requests for information on *named subjects.*

The assigning of such headings and references for incorporation into library catalogues is usually called *subject cataloguing.*

Subject cataloguing forms an integral part of the total cataloguing process and any distinction between this and other aspects of cataloguing must be somewhat artificial. However, given the limitations of this programmed course, it is necessary for us to concentrate, almost exclusively, on the problems of subject cataloguing.

From this viewpoint we shall examine, in some detail, the construction of two types of catalogue or index—the classified catalogue and the alphabetical subject catalogue.

In both cases we shall consider the application of the techniques of chain procedure to the construction of these catalogues. Chain procedure is most certainly not the only method available for subject catalogue construction. However, it does provide a very useful approach to examining basic principles in the construction of subject catalogues, and for this reason it is used in this course. An appreciation of chain procedure is a valuable background to the understanding of other methods, eg PRECIS and the use of lists of subject headings, consideration of which lies outside the scope of this particular volume.

Continue on frame 270

SECTION 3: THE CLASSIFIED CATALOGUE/PART I

The classified catalogue consists traditionally of three separate parts, namely
1 The classified file.
2 The alphabetical subject index to the classified file.
3 The author index.

In this section of the course our attention will be focused principally on the alphabetical subject index to the classified file and the techniques employed in its construction. We shall be particularly concerned with the method of index construction called *chain indexing*.

Before we proceed to examine chain indexing in any detail, we shall briefly describe the three parts of the classified catalogue. Each of these has its own particular functions and all are closely interrelated. Although we must concentrate on only one aspect of the construction of the classified catalogue, it is important to bear in mind the total structure of this kind of index.

Continue on the next frame

The AUTHOR INDEX

The author index, or 'author/title index', of a classified catalogue consists of entries and references arranged in alphabetical order of author and, where required, title, translator, series, etc, headings.

In the conventional card catalogue it will thus consist of a single alphabetical sequence of 5 x 3 inch cards.

This index therefore allows for the retrieval of documents via known authors, titles, translators, series, etc. It caters for what is commonly termed the *'author approach'* to information retrieval.

Once the searcher has located the relevant entry in the author index, the document can be retrieved from its position in a classified shelf arrangement by means of the call mark included in the entry for that document.

The problems which arise in making entries and references for the author index, ie the problems of *'author/title cataloguing',* lie outside the scope of this present course.

Continue on the next frame

272 (271)

The CLASSIFIED FILE

The classified file and its alphabetical subject index provide for what is commonly termed the *'subject approach'* to information retrieval. It is these two parts of the classified catalogue that are therefore our prime concern.

Entries made for documents in the classified file are arranged in a *classified order of subjects.* This classified order is determined by the scheme used for the classification of the documents. In this course we shall consider classified catalogues in which UDC is the scheme employed.

You have already had practice in classifying documents by UDC. In the construction of a classified catalogue the class number you assign to a document forms the *heading* for that document's entry in the classified file. Consequently the class number will determine the precise location of that entry in the overall classified arrangement of subjects.

Entries in the classified file are thus arranged, or filed, according to the notation of the classification scheme in use.

The UDC notation uses, in part, arabic numerals and these possess an *ordinal value.* With such symbols we thus have a ready-made *filing order,* 534 files before 535, 535.3 files before 535.4 and so on.

The notation, however, also employs symbols which normally have *no* ordinal value, such as + (plus sign), : (colon), / (oblique stroke) and - (hyphen).

When such symbols are used in a class number a decision must be made as to whether, for example, 534/535 files before or after 534 + 536. In other words, these symbols, / + ( ) etc, are *assigned* an ordinal value within the filing order of the elements in the notation.

On page 10, paragraph 6, of the scheme you can find a statement of the UDC filing order exemplified by class 675 Leather industry.

It is not necessary for you to commit this filing order to memory as you will not be required to employ it. You will not be required to *file* catalogue entries for documents classified by UDC as part of this course. Nor will you be required to arrange such documents on the shelves of a library.

The filing order of the notation is designed to maintain the desired order of *subjects* both on the shelves (ie the documents themselves) and in the classified file (ie the entries for those documents). You will remember that a notation *only maintains an already preferred order*, it does not *determine* it. This order is based on conceptual relations.

In our examination of the structure of the classified catalogue the *citation order* of concepts in a compound class number is of much greater significance that the filing order of the notation. This will become more evident as we proceed.

At this stage it is sufficient for you to bear in mind that, within any given class, the order of entries in a classified file is determined by

1 The *citation order* of concepts in the heading for a compound subject (ie in a compound class number)

2 The *filing order* between such headings

The order of entries in a classified file is not simply a duplicate of the order of documents on the shelves.

To begin with the classified file presents a *single* classified sequence whereas shelf order is often broken into *several* classified sequences by such factors as the physical form of documents, eg one sequence for books, another for pamphlets, etc.

Moreover, it is possible for a document to have *more than one entry* in the classified file whereas it can only have one physical location on the shelves.

Initially, however, we shall consider the classified catalogue which, *as a general rule,* contains only one entry for each document in the classified file. *This is called a single entry system.*

This single entry is filed under the class number which denotes the *specific summarisation* of the subject content of that document. It is a *specific subject entry.*

The classified file is thus a classified arrangement of subjects contained within documents possessed by the library. It is not a simple repetition of shelf order in the form of document substitutes.

The prime aim of the classified file is to facilitate the retrieval of information about *named subjects,* not the retrieval of named documents.

It achieves this aim principally through the *juxtaposition* of related subjects in a *classified order.*

Continue on the next frame

The *ALPHABETICAL SUBJECT INDEX*

In order to discover what information the library possesses about a particular subject, we must first locate that subject within the classified file. The entries under this subject will describe individual documents and tell us precisely where they can be found upon the shelves.

We have seen, however, that the entries in the classified file are arranged by the notation of the classification scheme. That is, they are arranged in an order that users cannot be expected to be familiar with. Thus entries about, say, town planning are *not* filed under the term 'town planning'. They are filed under the notation for this subject, 711.4.

Obviously all requests for information about subjects are couched, initially, in *natural language*, ie in *words* which *name* those subjects. A library user requests information about 'town planning' not about '711.4'. Nor does he know that 711.4 is the notational expression of this subject and that, therefore, relevant information will be filed under this class number in the classified file.

Thus, to locate a particular subject within the classified file, the statement of that subject in verbal terms must be *translated* into the statement of that subject in notational terms. The *name* of the subject must be translated into its *class number* which determines its location in the classified sequence of subjects.

The first function of the alphabetical subject index to the classified file is to provide for the approach to subjects via their names. Subjects are stated in verbal terms and provided with their corresponding class numbers. By translating the names of subjects into their notations, the alphabetical subject index serves as a key to the locations of subjects within the classified file.

The entries made in the alphabetical subject index do *not* refer to individual documents.

They contain only the names of *subjects* and their corresponding notations.

These entries are then filed in *alphabetical order* of subject names.

Let us consider our example of the subject *town planning*. An entry in the alphabetical subject index for this subject will consist solely of the name of the subject and its class number, thus

     Town planning   711.4

This entry will file in the alphabetical subject index as illustrated in the following diagram.

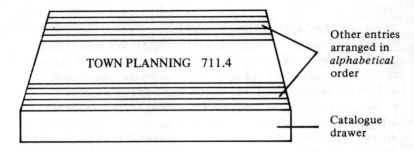

Other entries
arranged in
alphabetical
order

Catalogue
drawer

When a catalogue user wants to discover what documents the library contains about town planning, he first consults the *alphabetical subject index* under this *subject*. This tells him that the class number for town planning is 711.4.

He then consults the *classified file* at 711.4. Here he will find entries for the individual *documents* about town planning which have been assigned the class number 711.4 and filed under this heading.

Suppose, for example, that the library possesses the book by Thomas Sharp titled *'Town planning'*. The entry for this particular document will be filed in the classified file as illustrated below. Guide cards help to break up the classified sequence and direct the user to the required class as indicated.

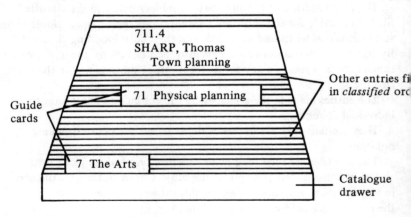

Guide cards

Other entries fi
in *classified* or

Catalogue
drawer

Continue on the next frame

274 (273)
From this point on in the course we shall be principally concerned with
the making of entries for subjects in the alphabetical subject index to
the classified file.

At this stage it might therefore be useful to summarise what has been
said so far about the classified catalogue as a whole.

SUMMARY
1 The classified catalogue consists traditionally of three separate parts,
   i   The author index
   ii The classified file
   iii The alphabetical subject index to the classified file
2 The classified file and the alphabetical subject index together facilitate
the retrieval of information about named subjects. As such they are our
chief concern in this course.
3 The classified file consists of entries for documents arranged in a classified sequence according to the notation of the classification scheme in use.
4 Before discovering what documents the library possesses about a
particular subject we must therefore know the class number for that
subject.
5 The alphabetical subject index provides this information. It consists of
entries, arranged in alphabetical order, stating the names of subjects and
giving their corresponding class numbers.
6 In the search for information about a named subject the user
   i   consults the alphabetical subject index under the verbal statement
      of that subject and is informed of its class number.
   ii consults the classified file under this class number and finds there
      entries for documents about the desired subject.
   iii each of these entries in the classified file will describe an individual
      document and tells the user precisely where in the library it is
      shelved.
Continue on the next frame

CHAIN INDEXING

So far we have established that the first function of the alphabetical subjec
index is to act as a key to the location of subjects in the classified file. It
does this by translating the names of subjects into their corresponding
notational expressions or class numbers.

The alphabetical index to the schedules of a classification scheme
performs a similar function. It acts as a key to the location of subjects in
the schedules, as you know from your practical classification.

Why bother, then, to create an alphabetical index to the classified file
when you already have a printed alphabetical index to the schedules of
the classification scheme?

The answer lies in the fact that the subjects within the classified file
are the subjects of actual documents in a particular collection. Thus the
alphabetical index to the classified file is an index to the subjects held in
this collection. The purpose of the classified file and its index is to
facilitate the retrieval of these documents in response to requests for
information on named subjects.

The alphabetical index to the schedules of a classification scheme,
however, is an index to *all* the subjects listed in the schedules. It is not an
index to the subjects of particular documents.

An attempt to use the alphabetical index to the schedules as an index
to the classified file would be unhelpful for two reasons.

1 Many of the subjects listed in the alphabetical index to the
schedules would not be represented in the collection of documents and
therefore would not be in the classifed file.

In such cases consultation of the classified files would be pointless
and frustrating to the user.

2 Many of the compound subjects of the documents in the collection,
represented by compound class numbers in the classified file, would not be
catered for in the alphabetical subject index to the schedules.

In such cases the user would be unable to gain immediate access to
the *specific* subject of his search.

It is thus essential for the indexer to create an alphabetical subject
index to the classified file. He does this by making the required alphabetical subject index entries as he classifies each document added to the
collection.

Continue on the next frame

276 (275)

The subjects named in the alphabetical (from now on shortened to A/Z) subject index to the classified file are the subjects of documents.

As you are aware, the subjects of most documents are *compound subjects*. Compound subjects contain two or more elements. They therefore contain two or more *terms* in their names.

For example, the subject *'Geomorphology of glacial landforms in Scotland'* contains four terms,

   geomorphology : landforms : glacial : Scotland

Now there is no one correct or accepted way of naming such a subject as this. These four terms might occur in *any order* in a verbal statement of this subject. Consequently, the catalogue user searching for information about this subject might formulate his request in any one of the possible permutations of these four terms.

He might consult the A/Z index under *any one* of the four terms and reasonably expect to be lead to the specific subject of his search in the classified file.

The problem posed in the naming of most compound subjects for retrieval purposes is that the searcher may begin his search by any one of several terms constituting the verbal statement of that subject.

Thus the A/Z subject index must provide entries that cater for these different approaches to the subject. It must at least provide entries in which each of these terms forms the *lead term*. The lead term is the term under which the entry files and by which it is therefore sought. Moreover these entries must ultimately direct the searcher to his desired specific subject in the classified file.

In the case of most compound subjects the provision of entries for all the *permutations* of their constituent terms would result in a quite impossible number of entries in the A/Z subject index.

There are several alternatives to permutation. One very economic and systematic method is known as *CHAIN INDEXING*.

It is to this method that we now turn our attention.
Continue on the next frame

The procedures of chain indexing are based upon the class assigned to a document.

The class number is a notational statement of the subject of the document. It defines the location of this subject within the classified files and therefore the location of entries for documents written *about* this subject.

Remember that we are concerned with a classified catalogue employing a *single entry system.* That is, as a general rule, each document is assigned only *one* class number which represents a *specific summarisation* of the subject of the document. This class number provides the heading for the *single specific subject entry* for the document in the classified file.

The structure of every class can be analysed into a 'chain' of concepts.

Take for example a document titled *'The Conservative case'.*

Subject analysis Politics/Political parties/UK/Conservative
Class number   329 (41-4) 11

The chain of this class can be written down as follows:

3	Social sciences
32	Political science.
329	Political parties.
(4)	Europe
(41-4)	United Kingdom (of GB and N Ireland)
11	Conservative party

The analysis of a class into its chain is done by consulting the schedules of the classification scheme and writing down *each step of division* within that class, as exemplified above.

Each chain thus reflects the successive application of the *characteristics of division* in a given citation order.

Concepts in chain order are therefore in an order of *successive subordination.*

Chain indexing is so-called because, by this method, the *lead term* in each alphabetical index entry for a given subject is systematically chosen from the *chain* of concepts present in the class assigned to that subject.
Continue on the next frame

Now let us look at the construction of index entries for a particular subject by chain indexing procedure.

With any given class number, the *first* alphabetical index entry made for that subject commences, or *leads* with the last term in the chain and qualifies this with the minimum number of superordinate terms that are necessary to indicate *its precise context.*

Take our example *'The Conservative case'.*

Class no	329 (41-4) 11	
Chain	3	Social sciences
	32	Political science.
	329	Political parties.
	(4)	Europe
	(41-4)	United Kingdom (of GB and N Ireland)
	11	Conservative party

The first alphabetical subject index entry made for the subject of this document is,

Conservative party : United Kingdom 329 (41-4) 11

We have constructed this index entry by taking the term for the *last* concept in the chain, Conservative party, as the *lead* term. In this case it is probably only necessary to qualify this term by the superordinate term, United Kingdom, in order to place it in its precise context.

Suppose the searcher, looking for information upon the subject of this document, consults the alphabetical subject index under this entry. Which of the following statements will then be true?

He will be lead *directly* to the location of the
specific subject of his search in the classified file. — frame 284

He will *not* be lead *directly* to the location of the
specific subject of his search in the classified file. — frame 287

279 (285)

You say that this A/Z index entry will direct him *at once* to the specific subject he is looking for. No. You must consider the problem more carefully.

We have already established that the index entry

      Conservative party : United Kingdom : 329(41-4)11

directs the searcher *at once* to the location of his specific subject.

In this instance, however, although our searcher is looking for informatic about the same subject, he has not consulted this A/Z subject index entry. To all intents and purposes he is unaware of its existence. He has approached his subject under the perfectly acceptable and predictable term *'Political parties'* and has found an A/Z index entry under this term.

Please turn to frame 285. Look carefully at the *exact* form of the A/Z subject index entries made. Then select the correct answer to the question and proceed with the course.

---

280 (281)

You think that concepts distributed in the classified file are also distributed in the A/Z subject index. This is not so.

You think that the concept Poetry, for example, which constitutes a distributed relative in the classified file, by virtue of the citation adopted in the classification of documents, is also distributed throughout the A/Z subject index.

Please return to frame 281 and look at the two specific A/Z index entries for class numbers 820-1 and 840-1. Remember that those entries file in *alphabetical order.*

Then reconsider the question carefully and proceed with the course.

You say that the concepts appear in a reverse order of the citation order employed in the class number. Correct.

In the verbal subject statement of the A/Z index entry

Conservative party : United Kingdom : 329(41-4)11

the concept Conservative party is cited *before* United Kingdom. In the class number for the subject it is cited *after* United Kingdom.

By qualifying lead terms, when necessary, by *superordinate* terms from the chain, we are *reversing* the citation order employed in the class number being indexed.

Why bother to reverse the citation order, why not employ the same citation order as the class number?

Let us consider two fairly straightforward subjects this time from class 8, Literature.

1 *'English poetry'*
   Class number   820-1
   Chain   8   Literature. Belles lettres
                  820   English literature
                  -1   Poetry
2 *'French poetry'*
   Class number   840-1
   Chain   8   Literature
                  840   French literature
                  -1   Poetry

The two specific A/Z subject index entries for these subjects are,

1 Poetry : English literature   820-1
   Poetry : French literature   840-1

These two entries will file in close proximity in the alphabetical sequence.

Now, by virtue of the citation order adopted in class 8, 'poetry' constitutes a distributed relative in the classified file. It is distributed under the various languages, English, French, etc, which appear earlier in the citation order.

Look at the two examples above and then decide which of the following statements you think is true.

Concepts distributed in the classified filed are
gathered together in the A/Z subject index   – frame 288
Concepts distributed in the classified file are also
distributed in the A/Z subject index   – frame 280

282   (285)

Your answer: This A/Z index entry will not direct him *at once* to the specific subject he is looking for. Correct.

Only the *specific* A/Z subject index entry provides direct access to the *full class number* for the subject, in this instance 329(41-4)11.

If the user happens to formulate his request at a more general, less specific level he will consult the A/Z subject index under an entry made for one of the superordinate terms in the chain.

eg	Political parties	329
or	United Kingdom : Political parties	329 (41-4)

In such cases he is directed *only part of the way* to the location of the specific class he really wants.

Nevertheless, providing that he has consulted the A/Z index under *any one of the terms in the chain*, he is at least directed to a relevant part of the classified file near to the location of the subject of his search.

Admittedly, this relevant part of the classified file may not be the specific class he wants. For instance, if he looks under *Political parties* he will be directed to 329, if under *United Kingdom : Political parties* to 329(41-4). In fact he needs to arrive at class 329(41-4)11 before his request is satisfied.

However, on arriving at one of these less specific classes, the classified order of entries in the classified file will lead him successfully to the specific class he desires, ie to class 329(41-4)11. The provision of *'guide'* or *'feature'* cards, displaying class numbers and their verbal translations, break up the classified sequence into manageable proportions and help in the process of guiding.

Thus, at whatever 'level' of the chain of concepts the user chooses to consult the A/Z subject index, on entering the classified file the classified order of subjects will guide him to the specific subject of his search.

We can see, then, that the series of entries produced by chain indexing procedure allows the user to gain access to the desired specific subject in the classified file by consulting the A/Z subject index under any one of that subject's constituent terms.

Continue on the next frame

So the order of subjects in the classified file and the order of subjects in the A/Z subject index are *complementary*. Let us look at the relationship between these two orders a little more closely.

We said that concepts in *chain order* are in an order of *successive subordination*. Take the chain of concepts in the subject represented by our class number 329(41-4)11 once more.

3	Social sciences
32	Political science.
329	Political parties.
(4)	Europe
(41-4)	United Kingdom (of GB and N Ireland)
11	Conservative party

When we analyse a class number into its chain, as above, we reveal the *citation order* of concepts employed in that class number.

As you already know, concepts which appear after the first cited concept constitute *distributed relatives*.

Distributed relatives are scattered to varying degrees in the classified file.

Their position within any given class, and therefore the degree of scatter to which they are subjected, is determined by their position in the citation order of concepts within that class.

In class 32, for instance, individual political parties, eg Conservatives, will be subjected to a greater degree of scatter than individual countries eg United Kingdom. Individual political parties appear later in the citation order, and 'lower' in the chain order of a class number, than do individual countries.

We said that, when the lead term in an A/Z subject index entry requires qualification in order to indicate its precise context, this qualification is provided by the minimum number of appropriate superordinate terms from the chain.

eg   Conservative party : United Kingdom 329(41-4)11

In an A/Z subject index entry such as this, in which order are the concepts cited in the verbal statement of the subject?

In the same order as the citation order employed
in the class number   — frame 286
In a reverse order of the citation order employed
in the class number   — frame 281

You say that the searcher will be lead *directly* to the location of the specific subject of his search in the classified file. Correct.

The index entry consulted is

Conservative party : United Kingdom 329 (41-4) 11

The searcher is looking for information about the Conservative party in the United Kingdom and this A/Z subject index entry directs him to class number 329(41-4)11 in the classified file.

Here he will find filed entries for documents about this subject. He will find entries for documents about the *specific subject* of his search eg *'The Conservative case'*.

Thus the first A/Z index entry made for a subject gives the searcher *direct* access to the full class number for that subject.

It is called the *specific A/Z subject index entry*.

The specific A/Z subject index entry for class 329(41-4)11 is

Conservative party : United Kingdom 329(41-4)11

Continue on the next frame

In providing the specific A/Z subject index entry we have by no means provided for *every* possible approach to the specific subject.

The person searching for information about the Conservative party in the United Kingdom might well begin by consulting the A/Z subject index under such terms as *United Kingdom, Politics* or *Political parties.*

Requests for information about a subject are often formulated in more general terms than the statement of the specific subject. The user may approach his subject at a number of different *levels* and by a number of different *terms.*

So far we have only provided for the user who happens to consult the A/Z subject index under the term *Conservative.*

Consequently, every appropriate term in the chain is indexed as a *lead term* qualified by such superordinate terms as are necessary to set it in its context. This is to make sure that, no matter what level the searcher begins at, the term appropriate to that level can be located in the A/Z subject index.

Each lead term is indexed to the class number appropriate to its level in the conceptual chain.

Take again our subject represented by the class number 329(41-4)11 analysed in the chain

3	Social sciences
32	Political science.
329	Political parties.
(4)	Europe
(41-4)	United Kingdom (of GB and N Ireland)
11	Conservative party

The specific A/Z subject index entry is

    Conservative party : United Kingdom   329(41-4)11

The procedure of chain indexing would generate *at least* the subsequent index entries:

United Kingdom : Political parties	329(41-4)
Europe : Political parties	329(4)
Political parties	329
Political science	32
Social sciences	3

Other problems raised by this example will be dealt with as you proceed with the course and refine the procedures of chain indexing.

Suppose the searcher looking for information about the Conservative party in the United Kingdom consults the A/Z subject index under the term *Political parties.*

Which of the following statements is true?

This A/Z index entry will direct him *at once* to the
specific subject he is looking for — frame 279

This A/Z index entry will not direct him *at once*
to the specific subject he is looking for — frame 282

---

286 (283)

You think that the concepts in the verbal subject statement are cited in the *same order* as in the class number for this subject.

No, this is not true.

Return to frame 283 and look at the analysis of class number 329(41-4) carefully. Surely the concept Conservative party appears *last* in the citation order of this class number.

Examine the A/Z subject index entry in question and the citation order employed in the *verbal statement* of the subject in this entry.

Then select the correct answer and proceed with the course.

You think that the searcher will not be lead *directly* to the location of the specific subject of his search in the classified file. No, you are wrong.

Remember that our hypothetical searcher is looking for information about the specific subject *Conservative party in the United Kingdom* and that entries for documents about this particular subject are located in the classified file under the class number 329(41-4)11.

Before his search can be successfully concluded he must arrive at this point in the classified order of subjects. To this end he must first consult the A/Z subject index in order to translate a verbal statement of his subject into a class number.

Now please return to frame 278. Look carefully at the class number for the document, its chain and the construction and form of the A/Z subject index entry in question.

Then select the correct answer to the question and proceed with the course.

You think that concepts distributed in the classified file are gathered together in the A/Z subject index. You are right.

The concept 'poetry', for example, is distributed in the classified file. Nevertheless, the searcher is able to go to the *single location* within the A/Z subject index, ie he can consult this index under the term 'poetry', and find there entries which serve as a key to the several locations of this concept in the classified file.

    eg   Poetry : English literature   820-1
           Poetry : French literature   840-1

By *reversing* citation order and then arranging the resulting verbal subject statements in alphabetical order, the A/Z subject index collects together those concepts which have been scattered in the classified file by virtue of the citation order employed in classifying.

Thus, in addition to serving as a key to the location of subjects in the classified file the A/Z subject index has as its second major function the *collocation of distributed relatives.*

If concepts in the A/Z subject index entries were listed in the *same citation order* employed in the classification of these subjects the result would be much less helpful. The index would then simply *repeat* an order already present in the classified file, it would not *complement* it.

The repetition of the citation order of the class number would result in A/Z subject index entries such as the following:

      Literature   8
      Literature:English   820
      Literature:English:Poetry   820-1
      Literature:French   840
      Literature:French:Poetry   840-1

In addition to simply repeating an order to be found in the classified file, all these entries would file under the *same* term 'Literature'.

We should *not* have provided for access to subjects by each of their constituent terms and there would be *no* collocation of distributed relatives.

Continue on the next frame

Before examining the practical procedures of chain indexing in more
detail in the second part of this section, we shall briefly summarise the
main points made so far concerning this method.

SUMMARY

1 Chain indexing provides a systematic and economic method of selecting
A/Z subject index entries for compound subjects.

2 The index entries made for a given subject are based upon the *chain*
of concepts present in the class assigned to that subject.

3 The *specific A/Z subject index entry* is constructed by *leading* with the
last term in the chain and qualifying this by the minimum number of
superordinate terms required to indicate its precise context.

The specific A/Z subject index entry directs the searcher to the *full
class number* for the subject.

4 Index entries are then made for *each* of the other terms in the chain
that are liable to be *sought* by the user looking for information about the
specific subject.

In each entry the lead term is qualified by the minimum number of
superordinate terms and indexed to the class number appropriate to its
level in the chain.

5 The series of A/Z index entries so produced allows the searcher to
gain access to the location of the specific subjects in the classified file
via *any one* of the potentially sought terms in the chain.

If he consults the specific index entry he is lead *directly* to the specific
subject in the classified file.

If he consults one of the other entries he is lead to a part of the classified file near to the subject of his search and the classified order of subjects
then guides him to the specific subject.

6 By chain indexing procedure, the verbal subject statement in each A/Z
index entry *reverses* the citation order employed in the class number for
that subject. The A/Z subject index thus provides an order of subjects
which *complements* that in the classified file and effects the *collocation
of distributed relatives*.

The following is an illustration of chain indexing applied to our fairly
straightforward example of the document about *'English poetry'*.

Title	*'English poetry'*	
SA	Literature/English/Poetry	
Class number	820-1	
Chain	8	Literature
	820	English literature
	-1	Poetry

A/Z subject index entries

Poetry : English literature	820-1
English literature	820
Literature	8

Now proceed with the second part of this section on the next frame.

SECTION 3: THE CLASSIFIED CATALOGUE/PART II

So far we have looked at the structure of the classified catalogue with
particular reference to the structure of the A/Z subject index as the key
to the location of subjects in the classified file. We have also considered
the basic principles of chain indexing, an economic and systematic
method of selecting entries for the A/Z subject index.

We shall now go on to examine in more detail the practical procedures
involved in making A/Z subject index entries by the chain indexing
method for the subjects of particular documents.

As you read through the subsequent pages you should always bear
in mind that an A/Z subject index entry is only made if it helps the
user locate the desired subject in the classified file.

The procedures of chain indexing which we shall now describe help
to ensure that the resulting index entries fulfil this criterion.

Continue on the next frame

Having classified a document, the first stage in chain indexing is to analyse the class assigned to that document in order to reveal its *conceptual chain,* ie the chain of concepts which go to form the subject of the document.

This analysis must always be carried out by consulting the *schedules* of the classification scheme.

We are analysing a *subject* not a class number. We must state *every step of division* in that subject and we can by no means rely on the class number itself to reveal these steps.

Moreover, each step of division should be stated, as far as possible, by a *single word.*

Eg	Subject	'Secondary schools'	
	Class no	373.5	
	Chain	3	Social sciences
		37	Education
		373	Secondary
		373.5	Schools

These points will be further developed as you proceed with the course.

Suppose you have classified, by UDC, the document *'Select methods of metallurgical assaying',* class number 669.9.

The first step in the chain of this class is,

    6 Technology

Now write down the complete analysis of the conceptual chain of this class by consulting the UDC schedules and stating each step of division by a single word. Then turn to frame 299.

Your answer:

     Assaying : Metallurgy   669.9

Quite right.

    The specific index entry for 669.9 leads with the last term in the chain, 'assaying'. In this case the use of the superordinate term 'metallurgy' as the only qualifier is quite sufficient to indicate the precise subject context.

    This verbal statement of the specific subject is indexed to the full class number 669.9.

    We might note here that the qualification of lead terms by all the superordinate terms in the chain is in most cases unnecessary. While the resulting A/Z entries are not 'wrong', they tend to be clumsy. For example in the index entry

     Assaying : Metallurgy : Chemical technology   669.9

the terms 'chemical technology' add nothing of real value to the verbal statement of the specific subject 'assaying:metallurgy'. They are redundant in this particular subject context.

Continue on the next frame

Having made the specific A/Z index entry, we must now make an index entry for every other term in the chain which is liable to be sought by a user looking for information about this subject.

In other words, we must ensure that every *sought term* in the chain form the *lead term* in an A/Z subject index entry.

In each index entry the lead term is only qualified by superordinate terms if these are required to indicate its precise context. Qualification is always provided by the *minimum number* of necessary superordinate terms.

In each index entry the lead term is indexed to the class number appropriate to its level in the chain, ie to the class number which represents that particular verbal subject statement.

Here is the chain of class 669.9 once more.

6	Technology
66	Chemical
669	Metallurgy
669.9	Assaying

The first A/Z subject index made by chain procedure was the specific subject entry

Assaying : Metallurgy   669.9

Now we move up the chain providing index entries for each of the potentially sought terms.

Which of the following is therefore the next A/Z subject index entry constructed by chain procedure?

Metallurgy	669.9	– frame 312
Metallurgy : Assaying	669	– frame 303
Metallurgy	669	– frame 297

294 (309)
Your answer : 656.7, ie Air transport management.
The analysis of this chain should be as follows:

6	Applied sciences
65	Management
656	Transport
656.7	Air

Surely each of the above steps of division is expressed in the class number 656.7.

There is no hidden link.

Please return to frame 309 and consider the question once more. Remember to consult the schedules carefully when carrying out your analyses.

---

295 (305)
Your answer:

Yearbooks : Civil engineering   624(058)

Well, you *could* employ this entry and it does conform to the procedure of chain indexing.

However, this choice implies a decision to index *all* form concepts *directly* whenever they occur in the chain of a subject.

If you pause to think of *all* the form concepts, and *all* the possible subjects presented in those forms, you will soon realise that this policy would result in a massive and uneconomical number of rather unhelpful index entries.

Please return to frame 305 and read again the explanation of the use of *see references* and *blanket references*. Then select the correct answer to the question and proceed with the course.

296   (299)

Your answer:

Assaying : Metallurgy : Chemical technology   669.9

True, this is an acceptable A/Z index entry for this subject. It leads with the last term in the chain, qualifies this with superordinate terms and provides the full class number for the subject.

However, we did say that the lead term should always be qualified by the *minimum number of superordinate terms* required to indicate the precise subject context.

In the above entry the use of the qualifying terms 'chemical technology' can be regarded as redundant. They do not add anything of real value to the specific subject statement,

Assaying : Metallurgy   669.9

Please continue with the course on frame 293

Your answer:
     Metallurgy   669
Correct.

    Metallurgy is a sought term in the chain and the next one we would provide an index entry for. It does not require further qualification by superordinate terms to indicate its precise context and is indexed to the class number for this subject, ie to the class number appropriate to its level in the chain, 669.

    Here is the chain for class 669.9 again:

6	Technology
66	Chemical
669	Metallurgy
669.9	Assaying

    We have now provided two A/Z subject index entries according to chain procedure

    Assaying : Metallurgy   669.9
    Metallurgy   669

    The same procedure is used in constructing entries for the other potentially sought terms in the chain.

    Write down what you consider to be the A/Z subject index entries remaining to be constructed for this subject and then turn to frame 308.

Your answer: 656.1/.5 ie Land transport management.

The analysis of this chain should be as follows:

6	Applied sciences
65	Management
656	Transport
656.1/.5	Land

Surely each one of the above steps of division is expressed in the class number 656.1/.5.

Please return to frame 309 and consider the question once more. Remember to consult the schedules carefully when carrying out your analyses.

You should have arrived at the following analysis.

Class number 669.9

Chain	6	Technology
	66	Chemical
	669	Metallurgy
	669.9	Assaying

If you have a different answer check to see where you went astray. Have you omitted a step of division? Have you written down unnecessary terms from the schedules at any of the steps?

You are now ready to make the first A/Z subject index entry for this subject. This is the *specific A/Z subject index entry* as it directs the searcher *immediately* to the location of this specific subject in the classified file.

It is constructed by *leading* with the *last* term in the chain and qualifying this with the *minimum number of superordinate terms* necessary to indicate the precise subject context.

This verbal subject statement is indexed to the *full class number.*

Which of the following do you consider is the specific A/Z subject index entry for the subject represented by class number 669.9 constructed according to the above procedure?

Technology : Metallurgy : Assaying   669.9 − frame 304

Assaying : Metallurgy   669.9 − frame 292

Assaying : Metallurgy : Chemical technology 669.9 − frame 296

300 (315)
Your answer: the concept *'Senses'* constitutes a false link in the chain.
No, you are wrong.

The subject under consideration is *'The psychology of perception'*.
Your analysis of the chain should be as follows

1	Philosophy
159.9	Psychology
159.93	Senses
159.937	Perception

Surely the subordination of *'Perception'* to *'Senses'* could not be regarded as a case of *false subordination* in this conceptual chain.

Consequently 'Senses' does *not* constitute a 'false link' in the chain.

Please return to frame 315. Read what was said about false links again and then select another answer to the question.

---

301 (309)
Your answer 656.2 ie Railway transport management. Correct.

The analysis of this chain is as follows.

6	Applied sciences
65	Management
656	Transport
656.1/.5	Land
656.2	Railway

The step of division, 656.1/.5 Land transport, is not expressed notationally in the class number 656.2 and yet it constitutes one of the concepts in the chain of this subject.

It is therefore a *hidden link* in the chain and one that requires an A/Z subject index entry as follows:

Railway transport : Management	656.2
Land transport : Management	656.1/.5
Transport : Management	656
Management : Applied sciences	65
Applied sciences	6

Continue on the next frame

302 (301)

Inadequacies in the *specific A/Z subject index entry* made for a subject can also occur if the indexer bases his analysis solely on the *class number* for that subject.

The specific A/Z index entry must provide a verbal statement of the specific subject and direct the user *at once* to the location of this subject in the classified file.

It is constructed by *leading* with the *last* term in the chain.

Now suppose you classify the following document as stated below;

Title	'Natural history of the Weald'	
SA	Natural history/Gt Britain/Weald	
Class number	502(422)	
Chain	5	Science
	502	Natural history
	502(4)	Europe
	502(410)	Gt Britain
	502(420)	England
	502(422)	South-east

By leading with the last term displayed in this analysis we produce the index entry

South-east England : Natural history   502(422)

Does this index entry provide a verbal statement of the specific subject?

Yes   – frame 319

No   – frame 310

303 (293)
Your answer:

      Metallurgy : Assaying   669

No. This is decidedly wrong.

The lead term 'metallurgy' is all right but you have then gone on to qualify this by the *subordinate* term in the chain 'assaying' and indexed this to the class number 669.

The resulting A/Z subject index entry is wrong on two counts.

    1 The verbal subject statement repeats a citation order already present in the classified file.

    2 The class number 669 is *not* the class number for the subject metallurgy : assaying. The correct class number for this subject is 669.9 and access to it has already been provided for in the specific A/Z subject index entry

           Assaying : Metallurgy   669.9

Please return to frame 293 and read through the text again carefully; then select another answer to the question.

---

304 (299)
Your answer:

      Technology : Metallurgy : Assaying   669.9

No. This is most definitely wrong.

You have chosen an entry which leads with the first term in the chain and then qualifies this by successively *subordinate terms.*

Your verbal statement thus follows the *same* citation order as the class number. If entries were constructed by this method the A/Z subject index would simply repeat an order of subjects already to be found in the classified file.

Please return to frame 299. Look at the chain and then read through the chain indexing procedure described once more. Then select another answer to the question.

The A/Z subject index entries you should have derived from this chain are given below.

'*Three-dimensional cinematographic projection*'

Class number 778.554.1

Chain		
	7	Arts=Fine arts
	77	Photography
	778	(Special applications)
	778.5	Cinematography
	778.55	Film projection=Projection
	778.554	(Special methods)
	778.554.1	Stereoscopic=Three-dimensional

A/Z Subject index entries

Three-dimensional film projection	778.554.1
Stereoscopic film projection	778.554.1
Film projection	778.55
Projection : Cinematography	778.55
Cinematography	778.5
Photography	77
Arts, fine	7
Fine arts	7

Make sure that you have provided entries for synonyms and have omitted the unsought links in the chain.

The statement that all synonyms are indexed directly requires some qualification.

When the use of all synonymous terms as indexing terms would result in a massive, and thus uneconomic, duplication of A/Z subject index entries *see references* are employed to direct the user from the rejected term or terms to the chosen indexing term. In other words when the term represents a widely distributed concept.

Suppose, for example, that the indexer decides that the terms '*Great Britain*' and '*United Kingdom*' are to all intents synonymous. Then, instead of making all the many index entries required under Great Britain and repeating them under the term United Kingdom he would choose only one of these terms as an indexing term.

A *see* reference is then made from the rejected term to the chosen term eg

    Great Britain   *see* United Kingdom

A similar procedure is adopted when dealing with *form concepts*. Information about almost every subject could be presented in the form of, say, a *report*.

If we were to index all the subjects about which reports were written under the lead term report it would generate a lengthy sequence of entries all filed under the same term. Instead, a large scale saving of index entries is achieved by producing a *general* or *blanket* reference in some such form as the following:

> Reports   *see* names of individual subjects. The class number for the subject is subdivided by the notation (047) to indicate report.

Suppose you have to produce A/Z subject index entries by chain indexing procedure for the subject of the document '*A yearbook of civil engineering*'. The class number assigned is 624(058).

Analyse the chain of this class and then decide which of the following index entries you would employ

> Yearbooks : Civil engineering   624(058)   — frame 295
> Yearbooks *see* names of individual subjects   — frame 314

306 (315)
Your answer: Philosophy. Correct.

After editing, the analysis of the chain for the subject 'The psychology of perception' 159.937 would thus be as follows:

1	(Philosophy)
159.9	Psychology
159.93	Senses
159.937	Perception

We can regard Philosophy as a *false link* in the chain. The subordination of the contemporary scientific discipline of Psychology to Philosophy could now be regarded as a case of *false subordination*.

We should not now expect a user, searching for information about the *'Psychology of perception'*, to consult the index under Philosophy. This term would not therefore be indexed. Our edited chain would thus generate the following entries:

Perception : Psychology	159.937
Senses : Psychology	159.93
Psychology	159.9

Continue with the course on frame 320.

---

307 (311)
Your answer: Film projection.

Now if you think more carefully you must agree that someone searching for information about *'Three-dimensional cinematographic projection'* might consult the index under *'Film projection'*.

This then would *not* be considered an 'unsought' term in the chain.

An 'unsought' term is one which a user would rarely, if ever, think of consulting in the A/Z index when formulating his request for information about a particular subject.

Please return to frame 311 and reconsider the question. Then select another answer and proceed with the course.

308   (297)

You should have produced the following A/Z subject index entries:

    Chemical technology   66
    Technology   6

These two index entries provide for approaches via the two remaining sought terms in the chain and index each concept to its appropriate class number.

Let us now look at the completed set of A/Z subject index entries made by chain indexing procedure for the subject *'Select methods of metallurgical assaying'*:

Class number	669.9	
Chain	6	Technology
	66	Chemical
	669	Metallurgy
	669.9	Assaying
Index entries	Assaying : Metallurgy	669.9
	Metallurgy	669
	Chemical technology	66
	Technology	6

Continue on the next frame

We said earlier that the analysis of a class into its chain must always be carried out by consulting the *schedules* of the classification scheme.

This is to ensure that no important step of division, which may well represent a sought term, is omitted from the analysis.

As you know, concepts in chain order are in an order of successive subordination. They are arranged in a *hierarchical order.*

If the notation of a classification scheme is not strictly expressive of all hierarchical relationships, then it is possible that one, or more, of the concepts in the chain of a particular subject are *not* represented notationally in the class number for that subject.

Take, for example, the subject '*Christian dogma*'. The UDC class number for this subject is 23. By looking at this class number alone it would appear to have only two steps of division.

2   Religion

23   Dogma

However, if you consult the *schedules* for class 2 you will see that there are in fact *three* steps of division which go to form this class number for Christian dogmatics, namely:

2   Religion

22/28 Christian

23   Dogma

The step of division, 22/28 Christian religion, is *not expressed notationally* in the UDC class number 23.

It is, however, present in the *chain of the subject* represented by class number 23. This presence must be recognised, for it constitutes a sought term and must receive an A/Z subject index entry as follows:

Dogma : Christian religion   23

Christian religion   22/28

Religion   2

Steps of division which are not expressed in the class number, and yet constitute part of the chain, are known as 'hidden links' in the chain.

In order to ensure that all 'hidden links' are recognised in the analysis of a chain, this analysis must always be carried out by a careful consultation of the schedules, *not by reliance on the class number alone.*

Now consider the following three subjects and their respective UDC class numbers.

Air transport management   656.7

Railway transport management   656.2

Land transport management   656.1/.5

Analyse each of the subjects represented by these class numbers into their respective chains. Which one of these chains includes a hidden link?

656.7	– frame 294
656.2	– frame 301
656.1/.5	– frame 298

---

310 (302)

Your answer: the index entry

     South-east England : Natural history   502(422)

does *not* provide a verbal statement of the *specific subject.*

    You are right.

    The subject of this document is *specifically* about the natural history of the *Weald* and so the specific A/Z subject index entry should be

        Weald : Natural history   502(422)

    However, the concept 'Weald' is *not* specified in the class number 502(422). An analysis of this class number, *as it stands,* would not reveal this concept in the chain and thus the specific subject would receive no A/Z index entry. Its existence would remain unknown to the user.

    In order to ensure that we do in fact produce the specific A/Z index entry by chain procedure it is necessary to *extrapolate* (ie *extend*) the chain *verbally* as follows:

5	Science
502	Natural history
502(4)	Europe
502(410)	Gt Britain
502(420)	South-east
502(422)	Weald

    The need to extend the chain verbally arises when the classification scheme is *insufficiently detailed* to provide a *specific class number* for the subject.

    The situation will rarely arise with UDC *if* the scheme is applied to its *full capacity* by the use of verbal extensions to the class number itself.

    Thus, in the example, Natural history of the Weald, the full UDC class number would be, 502 (422 Weald), giving us the chain,

5	Science
502	Natural history
502 (4)	Europe
502 (410)	Gt Britain
502 (420)	England
502 (422)	South-east
502 (422 Weald)	Weald

However, UDC is by no means *always* applied to this degree of detail in libraries. In such situations verbal extensions to the *chain* are essential to ensure effective A/Z subject index entries.

Moreover, this point is of importance as regards the general principles of chain indexing.

The analysis of the chain is the analysis of the *subject itself*, not simply of the class number.

The schedules must always be consulted to ensure that a *full* analysis of the class is achieved, that *every step of division* in the chain is stated.

We said earlier that each step of division should be stated, as far as is possible, by a *single word*. The adoption of this procedure simplifies the process of chain indexing. Use of the terms displayed in the schedules can prove unnecessarily confusing and can lead to inaccurate A/Z index entries.

Consider again the example *'Railway transport management'*, UDC class number 656.2.

In the analysis of this chain we encounter some of the *composite headings* frequently used in the UDC schedules.

Take, for example, the heading for class 656. You will see the following display in the schedules:

    656   Transport and postal services

The concept 'postal services' is, in fact, specifically catered for at class 656.8:

    656.8   Mail. Post.

This concept plays no part in the chain of the subject represented by class number 656.2 *'Railway transport management'*.

It should be omitted from the analysis of the chain, thus:

    656   Transport.

Composite headings abound in UDC. When dealing with them you should always select the concept relevant to the chain you are analysing and express this, as far as possible, by a single word.

The copying of words and phrases from the schedules encourages the indexer to use them as they stand and so produce index entries under which the user would not think of looking. Not all classification schemes employ terms in their schedules that are intended as *indexing terms* for retrieval purposes.

An obvious example occurs in the Colon Classification in class 2, Library science, where the term in the schedules for 'special libraries' is *'business'*. No user would look under 'business libraries' when searching for information about 'special libraries'.

Such adjustments to terminology are best made in the initial analysis of the chain.

A more likely fault to arise from copying phrases out of the schedules is the construction of A/Z index entries which contravene chain indexing procedure.

Look, for example, at UDC class *343.19 Criminal courts and tribunals.* This verbal display in the schedules *might* lead to the A/Z index entry

Criminal courts   343.19.

However, as a subclass of 343, Criminal law, we require the entry

Courts : Criminal   343.19

To help ensure this entry, employing the desired citation order, the term 'courts' only should be used in the analysis of the chain at class 343.19.

Some concepts, of course, can only be expressed by more than one term, eg *'Current affairs'*. There is no single term which adequately expresses this concept.

Nevertheless, as a *general rule* for the analysis of a chain, the use of more than one term at any single step of division should only be tolerated if these terms are more or less synonymous. We shall return to the problem of synonyms shortly.

For the above reasons, we repeat that each step of division should be stated, as far as possible, by a *single word* in the analysis of a chain.
Continue on the next frame

311 (310)

The procedures mentioned so far have been directed towards a *complete analysis* of the chain of any given class. By following them, your initial analysis of a chain should be a full analysis and it should be written down in a form that helps to ensure effective and helpful A/Z index entries.

Obviously, A/Z subject index entries are only made if they help the user locate the desired subject in the classified file.

To further ensure that all the index entries generated by chain procedure are indeed helpful, the initial analysis of the chain *may* require *EDITING*.

This editing of the chain takes place *before* any A/Z subject index entries are made.

The analysis of a subject into its chain may well reveal one or more steps of division representing terms that would rarely, if ever, be consulted by a user looking for information about that subject.

These are referred to as *unsought terms* ie *not* liable to be consulted or 'sought', by a user.

Consider the following subject and its chain:

'*Three-dimensional cinematographic projection*'

Class number   778.558.1

Chain	7	Arts
	77	Photography
	778	Special applications
	778.5	Cinematography
	778.55	Film projection
	778.554	Special methods
	778.554.1	Stereoscope

Which of the following steps of division represents in your opinion an unsought term in this chain?

Cinematography   — frame 318
Special methods   — frame 316
Film projection   — frame 307

312 (293)
Your answer:
> Metallurgy 669.9

This is incorrect.

True, we do require an index entry for the term 'metallurgy', but to what class number do we index this term?

669.9 is *not* the class number for metallurgy. It represents the more specific subject *metallurgical assaying.*

Remember that, in each A/Z subject index entry, the verbal subject statement is indexed to its appropriate class number.

Please turn to frame 293 and read through the text again carefully; then select another answer to the question.

---

313 (315)
Your answer: the concept *'Psychology'* constitutes a false link in the chain. No, you are wrong.

The subject under consideration is *'The psychology of perception'.*
Your analysis of the chain should be as follows:

1	Philosophy
159.9	Psychology
159.93	Senses
159.937	Perception

The subordination of *'Senses'* to *'Psychology'* could hardly be regarded as a case of *false subordination* in this conceptual chain.

Consequently 'Psychology' does *not* constitute a 'false link' in the chain.

Please return to frame 315. Read what was said about false links again and then select another answer to the question.

314 (305)
Your answer:

Yearbooks *see* names of individual subjects

Correct.

In other words you would employ a *general* or *blanket reference* from a term denoting a form concept ie 'Yearbooks'.

Remember that *see* references are only used in the A/Z subject index when they result in a large scale saving of index entries.

The general rule is to index synonyms *directly*. By doing so we provide *direct* access to the classified file via all synonymous terms liable to be consulted by the user.

For this reason the recognition of synonyms is one of the procedures in the editing of the chain.

Continue on the next frame

---

315 (314)
The final aspect of editing the chain that we must consider is the recognition of any step of division manifesting a case of *false subordination*.

When a concept is falsely subordinated to another this must be regarded as a *fault* in the classification schedules.

Such faults might arise from a poor organisation of the schedules, or a mistake in the initial conceptual analysis or a failure to recognise a generally accepted change in the relationship between concepts.

Whatever the reason, a step of false subordination, revealed in the analysis of a chain, is referred to as a *false link* in the chain.

As such they would not be sought by a user looking for information about the specific subject and they would not receive index entries.

Consider the subject *'The psychology of perception'*, class number 159.937.

Analyse this class by reference to the schedules and then say which of the following concepts constitutes a false link in the chain in your opinion.

Senses   — frame 300
Psychology — frame 313
Philosophy — frame 306

316 (311)

Your answer: Special methods.

Correct. It is highly unlikely that any one would consult the A/Z subject index under the term 'Special methods'. This would therefore be regarded as an *unsought link* in the chain and would receive no index entry.

In fact this particular chain contains *two* unsought links. Having analysed the chain these would be noted in its editing by, for example, enclosing them in brackets as illustrated below.

This editing helps to ensure that the unsought links, or unsought terms, do *not* receive index entries and are *not* employed as qualifying terms.

Class number	778.554.1	
Chain	7	Arts
	77	Photographic
	778	(Special applications)
	778.5	Cinematography
	778.55	Film projection
	778.554	(Special methods)
	778.554.1	Stereoscopic

Continue on the next frame

317 (316)
This particular chain provides examples of another form of editing—the recognition of *SYNONYMS*.

The policy in the construction of the A/Z subject index is to index all synonymous or near synonymous terms *directly*. That is, we do not generally choose one term as an indexing term and then *refer* the user from synonymous terms to entries under the chosen term.

The use of such *see references* from a synonym to a preferred indexing term is restricted as it saves the user from having to consult *two* parts of the A/Z subject index *before* he is able to gain access to the classified file.

For example, taking the two terms *Disease* and *Pathology* we make such index entries as the following

     Disease : Medicine   616

     Pathology : Medicine   616

By providing index entries under *both* terms, the user can gain access to classified file directly by consulting either one of the terms.

He is *not* referred from, say, Pathology to Disease by the reference

     Pathology *see* Disease

before he can gain access to the relevant part of the classified file.

As we intend to provide A/Z subject index entries for synonymous terms, synonyms are indicated in the analysis of the chain by further editing.

This form of editing can be done by writing synonyms at their appropriate level of the chain and introducing them with an = (equals) sign.

Look again at the following chain. It has now been edited to recognise *unsought links* (in brackets) and *synonyms* (introduced by =).

    'Three-dimensional cinematographic projection'

Class number	778.554.1	
Chain	7	Arts = Fine arts
	77	Photography
	778	(Special applications)
	778.5	Cinematography
	778.55	Film projection = Projection
	778.554	(Special methods)
	778.554.1	Stereoscopic = Three-dimensional

Now write down what you consider to be the A/Z subject index entries derived from this edited chain. Then turn to frame 305.

318 (311)
Your answer: Cinematography.

Surely it is feasible that a person searching for information about the subject *'Three-dimensional cinematographic projection'* might consult the index under the term *'Cinematography'*.

If this is so then *'Cinematography'* would *not* be considered an 'unsought' term in the chain.

Remember than an 'unsought' term is one which a user would rarely, if ever, think of consulting in the A/Z index when formulating his request for information about a particular subject.

Please return to frame 311 and reconsider the question. Then select another answer and proceed with the course.

---

319 (302)
You think that the index entry provides a verbal statement of the specific subject. You must reconsider your decision.

The index entry in question is

South-east England : Natural history   502(422)

It is true that this provides a specific verbal statement of the subject expressed in the class number. But is it a verbal statement of the specific subject about which the document is written?

It is of vital importance that you do not confuse the two. In analysing a chain we are analysing a *subject,* not a class number.

Please return to frame 302. Look, more carefully, at the subject of the document. Then reconsider the question and proceed with the course.

320 (306)

The foregoing discussion of chain indexing has been set in the context of a classified catalogue employing, as a general rule, a *single specific subject entry* in the classified file for each document, ie a *single entry system.* Other systems are used, especially in classified catalogues employing UDC, but these will not be dealt with in this particular volume.

It was not our intention, nor indeed is it feasible, to cover every eventuality that will be encountered in producing A/Z index entries for the subjects of particular documents by chain indexing procedure.

You have, however, been introduced to the fundamental principles of chain indexing and, from the basis of this understanding, you should be in a position to deal with most of the problems liable to arise in practice.

We shall now summarise the main points made in the second part of this section of the course. You will then be required to produce A/Z subject index entries by chain procedure for the subjects of particular documents on your own.

SUMMARY

1 The analysis of a chain is the analysis of a *subject* not simply of a class number.

2 The analysis of a chain must therefore be carried out by a careful consultation of the *schedules* of the classification scheme.

3 This is to ensure that a *full analysis* is achieved, that *every step of division* is stated, including any

a)   *Hidden links*—intermediate steps of division not expressed in the class number.

b)   *Extensions to the chain*—where the class number is *not specific.*

4 Every step of division should be stated, as far as possible, by a *single term.*

5 This full analysis of the chain may then require editing in order to identify

a)   *Unsought links*—these *will not* receive index entries.

b)   *False links*—these *will not* receive index entries.

c)   *Synonyms*—these *will* receive index entries.

6 A/Z subject index entries can now be made for every term in the edited chain which is liable to be *sought* by a user looking for information about the specific subject.

7 In each case the lead term is qualified by the *minimum number* of necessary *superordinate terms* and is indexed to the class number appropriate to its level in the chain.

NB: Once an A/Z subject index entry has been made for a particular subject it need *never again* be repeated.

This fact tends to be lost sight of when considering chain indexing in isolation from the construction of an actual catalogue.

In this course, however, you are *not* concerned with the construction of an actual catalogue. Your concern is to practice the technique of chain indexing. You must treat each subject as a *separate entity* and produce A/Z subject index entries accordingly.

Continue on the next frame

---

321 (320)

As a conclusion to these sections dealing with the classified catalogue we offer the following exercise in the application of chain indexing procedure.

You have already provided a subject analysis and a UDC class number for each of the two following examples and these are repeated here for convenience.

1 *'Cereal diseases: Ministry of Agriculture, Fisheries and Food Bulletin No 129'*
SA: Agriculture/Cereals/Diseases
UDC 633.1-2

2 *'Library resources in the Greater London area: No 5 Agricultural libraries'*
SA: Library science/Special libraries/Agriculture/London
UDC 026:63(421)

For each of the above subjects would you now produce:

a)   an analysis of the chain

b)   A/Z subject index entries by chain indexing procedure

Check your answers with those provided on frame 354.

SECTION 4: THE ALPHABETICAL SUBJECT CATALOGUE

In the previous section of this course we were concerned with the classified catalogue. This type of catalogue consists, traditionally, of *three* separate parts—the author/title index, the classified file, and the A/Z subject index to the classified file.

The classified catalogue facilitates the retrieval of information about subjects through:

1 a classified arrangement of subjects in the classified file;
2 access to, and support of, this classified arrangement via the names of subjects arranged in alphabetical order in the A/Z subject index.

We must now turn our attention to the *alphabetical subject catalogue.* This type of catalogue, as its name implies, provides for the retrieval of information about subjects by *naming* subjects in *verbal statements* and arranging these subject names in *alphabetical order.*

There is *no* classified sequence of subjects in the alphabetical subject catalogue. It is often said that the basic theory of the alphabetical subject catalogue is the utility to the user of providing *direct access* to the *'known names'* of subjects (ie verbal statements) in a *'known order'* (ie alphabetical order). This, as we shall see, is a considerable oversimplification of the problem.

The problems of alphabetical subject cataloguing can be, and often are, demonstrated by reference to the *dictionary catalogue.*

The dictionary catalogue derives its name from the fact that it consists of a *single sequence* of entries and references filed in alphabetical order of headings.

All types of entry and reference—author, title, subject, series, etc—are *interfiled* in this one sequence which thus caters for *all* approaches to information retrieval.

In this particular course we are only concerned with catalogues as tools for the retrieval of information about named subjects ie the 'subject approach' to information retrieval. We are not therefore concerned with the dictionary catalogue in its totality.

Many 'dictionary' catalogues are, in fact, 'divided'. This is, the author/ title entries and references are filed in a separate sequence from the subject entries and references. These subject entries and references thus constitute an *alphabetical subject catalogue.*

From now on we shall refer exclusively to the alphabetical subject catalogue, named, for convenience, the *A/Z subject catalogue.*

In a library using an A/Z subject catalogue, a classification scheme is only used to determine the classified order of documents on the shelves. It is not used directly for the arrangement of document representations in the catalogue. The A/Z subject catalogue possesses no classified sequence of entries as is found in the classified file of a classified catalogue. It is composed entirely of entries and references arranged in an alphabetical order of subject names.

Subject cataloguing for the A/Z subject catalogue thus involves two fundamental activities:

1 the selection of *verbal subject headings* under which the entries for individual documents will file;

2 the construction of a system of *subject references* (cross-references) which is designed to guide the user from one subject heading to related subject headings under which relevant information, in the form of document entries, can be found. This makes up for the absence of a systematic sequence showing such connections.

The core problem, and the first with which we shall deal, is the selection of the *subject heading* for a document entry, ie the name of the subject about which the document is written.

Continue on the next frame

The subject heading under which the entry for a particular document files should be a *specific* description of the subject about which that document is written.

It is thus called a *specific subject heading.*

If a user consults the A/Z subject catalogue, *at his first approach,* under the specific subject heading which describes the subject of his search he will *immediately* discover what documents the library possesses containing information about that subject. The document entries filed under this subject heading contain the call marks for these documents telling the user where they can be located in the classified shelf arrangement.

For example, if the user wants information about *Town planning* and he consults the catalogue under this subject heading he will find there entries for documents about town planning, eg:

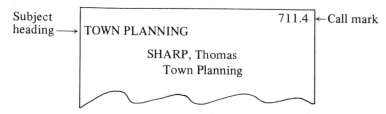

Subject heading ⟶ TOWN PLANNING   711.4 ←Call mark

SHARP, Thomas
Town Planning

Unlike the classified catalogue, where the user must first consult the A/Z subject index (only *references*) and only *then* go to the classified file of *full entries,* the A/Z subject catalogue theoretically provides *direct access* to entries for documents about named subjects.

However, to achieve this *direct* access, the user must locate the relevant specific subject heading at his *first* approach to the catalogue.

This assumes that he has formulated his request by:
1 naming the subject at the *specific level* desired;
2 naming this specific subject *in the same terms* used by the indexer;
3 citing these terms *in the same order* as they are cited in the specific subject heading.

Unless *all* these conditions are observed, access to a subject in the A/Z subject catalogue is *not direct* and a further search must be made via a *subject reference* of some kind. We shall deal with the problem of references later.

Now the majority of subject headings are statements of *compound subjects*. Such compound subject headings are composed of more *than one term*. As soon as we have more than one term in a heading, the decision as to the citation order of those terms is one of critical importance.

Obviously the *first cited term*, ie the *lead term* in the heading, determines where the subject heading will file in the alphabetical sequence of subjects and thus where it can be located.

The aim of a subject heading is that it should name the subject in the form *most likely to be sought* by a user.

However, in the case of many compound subjects there is *no* such obvious form of name. There is no *'known name'*.

Consider, for example, the subject *'The advertising of aluminium pressure-cookers on television'*.

This subject consists of the four elements

Advertising : Aluminium : Pressure-cookers : Television.

There is no *accepted name* for a compound subject such as this. There is no obvious *citation order* for its constituent terms. Different enquirers might ask for this subject in quite different ways—eg, Is there anything on *TV advertising of aluminium pressure-cookers?*

As we saw in the A/Z subject index to the classified catalogue, the attempt to provide for every possible approach to the citation order of terms in compound subjects by permuting the terms may lead to an unacceptable number of entries in the catalogue.

We must therefore attempt to select the chosen form of name ie the chosen form of the specific subject heading in the case of the A/Z subject catalogue.

As there are no rules in natural language that allow us to predict the one 'accepted' or 'sought' name for many compound subjects, we must inevitably look for other rules.

E J Coates, editor of the British Technology Index (an outstanding example of a *specific* A/Z subject index) has suggested a *'significance order'* of terms which helps us to determine the citation order in headings for compound subjects, at least up to a point.

This order is based on the *conceptual relationships* between the constituent elements of a compound subject.

You are already familiar with the idea that concepts can be regarded as manifestations of particular categories of concepts eg, Ranganathan's five Fundamental Categories P M E S T.

Coates uses different names for categories of concepts and suggests that the basic *significance order* is the citation order of categories

Thing → Material → Action. To this we can add the category Agents, giving us a *basic significance order* of

Thing → *Material* → *Action* → *Agent*

This must be supplemented by further rules for less obvious relations, but the above will take us a long way in solving the problem of citation order. However, it should be noted that such a significance order of catagories is more readily recognisable in, and applicable to, the disciplines of natural science and technology than to the social sciences, humanities and fine arts.

Now if we take that compound subject *'The advertising of aluminium pressure-cookers on television'* and cast its constituent concepts in the basic *significance order* Thing → Material → Action → Agent, we arrive at the following citation order:

Thing   Material   Action   Agent

Pressure-cooker : Aluminium : Advertising : Television

In this particular subject pressure-cookers constitute the 'Thing', aluminium the 'Material', advertising the 'Action', and television the 'Agent' through which the advertising is carried out.

Consider the subject *'Application of computers to the quality control of wool textiles'.*

If we cast the constituent concepts of this compound subject in the basic significance order of Thing → Material → Action → Agent, at which of the following citation orders do we arrive?

Wool : Textiles : Quality control : Computers   – frame 331

Textiles : Wool : Quality control : Computers   – frame 328

Computers : Textiles : Wool : Quality control   – frame 334

324 (340)

Your answer:

     Occupational diseases : Diagnosis.

Correct.

     In this compound subject 'occupational disease' is the *Thing*, 'diagnosis' is an *Action.* Consequently, by following the *significance order* we arrive at the above subject heading.

     If we had adhered strictly to the citation order prescribed by *chain procedure,* ie *lead* with the *last term* in the chain, qualified by *superordinate* terms, we would have produced the subject heading

     Diagnosis : Occupational diseases

     Neither of these headings is 'incorrect'. There is no 'correct' way of naming a compound subject such as this.

     The indexer's guiding principle is to produce a subject heading in the form 'most likely to be sought be a user'.

     This factor undoubtedly introduces an element of subjectivity on the part of the indexer in his selection of the citation order of terms in a compound subject heading.

     In the above example he must decide which of the headings is most likely to be sought by the user and there is no law to guide him.

     In your practical indexing in this course, the procedure you are required to follow in the selection of specific subject headings is this:

    1 Follow the citation order prescribed by *chain procedure* ie lead with the last term in the chain qualified by superordinate terms.

    2 Modify this order *only* when you think it generates a decidedly *unhelpful* subject heading.

    3 In such cases use the *basic significance order* Thing → Material → Action → Agent as your guide in determining the modified citation order of the compound subject heading.

     As we have said, this procedure involves a definite element of subjectivity in deciding just what is the most helpful citation order.

     However, once having made this decision, an essential factor is to ensure that the system of *subject references* leads the user to the chosen form of subject heading.

     It is in the construction of a system of references that chain procedure really plays a vital role and it is to this problem that we now turn our attention.

Continue with the course on frame 339.

325 (344)
Your choice:
    Diseases : Diagnosis *see also* Diagnosis : Diseases
No, you are wrong.
    This answer implies that you have used the heading
        Diagnosis : Diseases
under which to make entries for particular documents about this subject.
If there were no document entries under a heading you would not direct
a user to it via a *see also* reference.
    In fact you have rejected this particular heading in favour of one em-
ploying the citation order
        Diseases : Diagnosis
    Please return to frame 344. Look at the example carefully, then choose
the correct answer to the question.

---

326 (332)
You think that if we suppress a term in the specific subject heading then
the citation order in that heading follows the order prescribed by chain
procedure.
    No, this is not true.
    Remember that the citation order prescribed by chain procedure is a
citation order that leads with the last term in the chain.
    If we *suppress* or *subordinate* a term in specific subject heading we
remove that term from its lead position. We remove it from the position
prescribed by strict adherence to chain procedure order.
    Please return to frame 332. Read through the text carefully and look
at the example again. Then select the correct answer to the question and
continue with the course.

327   (329)

Your answer:

Metallurgy : Assaying

is the specific subject heading derived by chain procedure.

How can this be? Metallurgy is not the *last* term in this chain. The last term in the chain is Assaying and you have used this term to *qualify* Metallurgy.

Please return to frame 329. Read again about chain procedure in the selection of the *citation order* in compound subject headings. Then select another answer to the question and proceed with the course.

328 (323)

Your answer:

Textiles : Wool : Quality control : Computers.

Correct. This represents the basic significance order:

Thing $\rightarrow$ Material $\rightarrow$ Action $\rightarrow$ Agent

applied to the compound subject 'Application of computers to the quality control of wool textiles'.

Textiles are the Thing, wool the Material, out of which the Thing is made, quality control the Action and computers the Agent through which the Action is carried out.

The basic significance order is not sufficiently detailed to provide precise rules for the citation order in *all* compound subjects. For example we may well have more than one manifestation of the categories Thing, Material, Action or Agent in a given compound subject.

Coates has further refined this basic significance order by defining some twenty types of relationships between concepts in compound subjects and giving the suggested citation orders based upon these relationships. [See Coates, E J 'Subject catalogues: headings and structure'. Library Association, 1960.]

For the purposes of this course we do not intend to use this detailed analysis of citation orders based on the relationship between categories of concepts.

We shall base our procedure for the construction of subject headings upon the conceptual relationships expressed in *classification schemes*. This, however, is only one method available for the systematic selection of headings and we shall return to the basic significance order Thing $\rightarrow$ Material $\rightarrow$ Action $\rightarrow$ Agent later.

Continue on the next frame

CONSTRUCTION OF SUBJECT HEADINGS BY CHAIN PROCEDURE

It is possible to utilise the conceptual relationships expressed in a classification scheme in the selection of subject headings for document entries
in the A/Z subject catalogue, ie in the naming of subjects about which
the documents are written.

This method has the important added advantage, as we shall see, of
providing a system of *subject references* as well as giving us a citation
order for compound subject headings.

In our practical indexing we shall concentrate upon this method and
the classification scheme we shall refer to is UDC.

The technique is analagous to that already described for the constructic
of A/Z subject index entries in the classified catalogue and is similarly
based upon *CHAIN PROCEDURE.*

Having classified a document, the class to which the document has
been assigned is analysed into its *conceptual chain.*

Remember that this is an analysis of the *subject* itself, not of the class
number as it stands.

The analysis of the chain must be a *complete* analysis with every step
of division stated.

This complete analysis *may* then require various forms of *editing.*

These procedures have been dealt with in the previous section of this
course and will not be restated here.

The *specific subject heading* is then constructed in a way very similar
to that employed in constructing the specific A/Z subject index entry for
a classified catalogue by chain indexing procedure.

The *last* term in the chain provides the *lead term* (ie the first cited term
in the specific subject heading.

This is qualified by the *minimum number of superordinate terms*
necessary for a precise statement of the specific subject.

Let us consider again our fairly straightforward example *'Select method
of metallurgical assaying',* UDC class number 669.9.

Chain:	6	Technology
	66	Chemical
	669	Metallurgy
	669.9	Assaying

Which of the following is the specific subject heading for this subject
derived by chain procedure?

Metallurgy : Assaying	– frame 327
Assaying : Metallurgy	– frame 332
Assaying	– frame 335

330 (337)
Your answer:
  Slavery : Abolition *see* Abolition : Slavery
No, this reference would *not* appear.
  You have modified chain procedure order and *rejected* the heading
Abolition : Slavery.
  Then why make a *see* reference *from* a preferred *to* a rejected form of
heading?
  Return to frame 337 and read through the text once more. Then care-
fully consider the example before selecting the correct answer to the
question.

---

331 (323)
Your answer:
  Wool : Textiles : Quality control : Computers.
No, this is not correct.
  In this subject context the concept wool plays the role of Material. It
is the Material of which the Thing is constituted.
  If this is so then your citation order cannot conform to the basic signi-
ficance order
    Thing $\rightarrow$ Material $\rightarrow$ Action $\rightarrow$ Agent
  Please return to frame 323 and reconsider the question.

Your answer:

     Assaying : Metallurgy

Correct. This specific subject heading has been constructed by leading with the last term in the chain and qualifying this with the superordinate term 'metallurgy'. This verbal statement is sufficient to give us a precise statement of the specific subject.

    Strict adherence to the citation order prescribed by chain procedure can sometimes produce an obviously unhelpful citation order of terms in a compound subject heading.

    For example, if the *last* term in the analysis of the chain represents a *time* or *form* concept, then by strict adherence to chain procedure, this would constitute the *lead* term in the subject heading.

    However, entry under a time or form concept would rarely be helpful to the user and in such cases these terms are subordinated in the subject heading.

    Take, for instance, the subject of the document *'Conference proceedings on secondary education'.*

UDC class number	373 (063)	
Chain	3	Social sciences
	37	Education
	373	Secondary
	373 (063)	Conference proceedings

If we were to adhere strictly to the citation order prescribed by chain procedure, ie lead with the last term in the chain, we should arrive at the subject heading

    Conference proceedings : Secondary education

A much more helpful citation order for the subject heading is, however

    Secondary education : Conference proceedings

In other words we have *suppressed* the terms 'conference proceedings' in order to achieve a more helpful subject heading which leads with the terms 'secondary education'. (It may be remembered that such terms as 'Conference proceedings' do appear in the A/Z Subject Index to a classified file—but only as *general references* eg, Conference proceedings on particular subjects *see* name of subject.)

    If, as in the above example, we suppress a term in the specific subject heading which of the following statements is true?

    The citation order in the subject heading follows
    that prescribed by chain procedure.   — frame 326

    The citation order in the subject heading modifies
    that prescribed by chain procedure.   — frame 338

333 (338)

You say that the basic significance order referred to is

    Agent → Action → Material → Thing

No. In fact this is the *reverse* of the basic significance order.

    You should return to frame 323 and do some revision on the basic significance order.

Then continue with the course on frame 340.

---

334 (323)

Your answer:

    Computers : Textiles : Wool : Quality control.

No, this is not so.

    In this particular subject context computers do not constitute a Thing. They could represent this category in other subjects, eg *'The manufacture of computers'*, where they are the Thing being manufactured. In the subject in question, however, they represent an Agent facilitating the carrying out of an Action, namely quality control.

    Thus your citation order cannot conform to the basic significance order:

    Thing → Material → Action → Agent

Please return to frame 323 and reconsider the question.

---

335 (329)

Your answer:

    Assaying

is the specific subject heading derived by chain procedure.

    Assaying is the last term in the chain but it does not, by itself, provide a description of the *specific subject*. This is the aim of a *specific subject heading*.

    Please return to frame 329 and read carefully through the text once more. Then choose the correct answer to the question and proceed with the course.

Your answer:

     Higher education *see also* Education
     Education   *see also* Social sciences

No, this is an incorrect answer.

You were asked to select the references that lead *from* broader *to* narrower subjects.

Surely 'Higher education' is *narrower* in extent than 'Education' and 'Education' narrower than 'Social sciences'.

These are not therefore references that lead from broad subjects to narrower, more specific ones.

Please return to frame 339 and read through the text again, looking at the examples carefully. Then select the correct answer and proceed with the course.

337 (344)
Your answer:
      Diagnosis : Diseases *see* Diseases : Diagnosis
Quite right.
      The chosen specific subject heading modifies the citation order pre-
scribed by chain procedure. We must therefore provide a *see* reference
from the rejected form of heading *to* the chosen form of heading.
      If we failed to provide this see reference, the sought term in the chain
'Diagnosis' would not appear as a lead term in the system of references
generated for the specific subject.
      The rule thus established is, if the specific subject heading represents
a *modification* of the citation order prescribed by chain procedure, then
a *see* reference must be made *from the rejected heading,* ie that one
prescribed by chain procedure, *to the chosen heading.*
      Now the need to modify chain procedure order does not only occur at
the last step in a conceptual chain, ie in the creation of the specific
subject heading.
      This need may arise at any one of the superordinate steps in the chain,
ie in the creation of any one of the see also references leading to that
heading.
      Strict adherence to chain procedure may produce an unhelpful citation
order in any of the subject headings corresponding to superordinate
steps in the hierarchy.
      At whatever step you decide to modify chain procedure order to
produce a more helpful heading, you must ensure that a *see* reference
is made from the rejected to the chosen form of heading.
      Consider, for example, a document about *'The abolition of slavery
in the USA'.*
      UDC class number   326.8(73)
      The conceptual chain of this class is analysed below. The full subject
heading corresponding to each step in this chain is provided as the
preliminary stage in the construction of a *specific subject heading* and
a series of *specific references.*

      326.8(73)
      3   Social sciences   Social sciences
      32   Political science   Political science
      326   Slavery   Slavery
      326.8   Abolition   Slavery : Abolition
      326.8(73)   USA   Slavery : Abolition : USA

Which of the following references would appear in the system of references constructed?

Slavery : Abolition *see* Abolition : Slavery   — frame 330
Abolition : Slavery *see* Slavery : Abolition   — frame 346

---

338 (332)

You say that the citation order in the subject heading *modifies* that prescribed by chain procedure. You are quite correct.

Chain procedure tells us to *lead* with the *last* term in the chain. This would give us the subject heading:

Conference proceedings : Secondary education.

However, we consider that a more helpful subject heading is:

Secondary education : Conference proceedings.

By choosing this more helpful heading, which *suppresses* the form concept 'conference proceedings', we have altered, or *modified,* the citation order prescribed by chain procedure. We have *not* lead with the last term in the chain.

The practice of modifying the citation order prescribed by chain procedure can be extended beyond the suppression of time and form concepts to any situation in which the indexer considers that this citation order produces an unhelpful subject heading.

When such a cases arises in your practical indexing you are required to use the basic significance order, mentioned earlier, as a guide in determining the modified chain order.

This basic significance order based on categories of concepts is:

Agent → Action → Material → Thing   — frame 333
Thing → Material → Action → Agent   — frame 340

CONSTRUCTION OF SUBJECT REFERENCES BY CHAIN PROCEDURE

So far we have only considered the problem of selecting a specific subject heading. It is under the chosen form of heading that the catalogue entry for a particular document is filed and hence located.

However, unless a searcher looking for information about a specific subject formulates his request

1 at the *specific level* desired,

2 using the *same terms* as the indexer has used,

3 citing these terms in the *same order* as they are cited in the specific subject heading,

he will be unable (at least at first) to locate the relevant subject heading in the catalogue. He will not be able to retrieve documents relevant to his request.

Moreover, there is no *classified* arrangement of subjects in the A/Z subject catalogue. The only order of *names* of subjects by the letters making them up, is a relatively *arbitrary* order so far as bringing together related topics is concerned. Many of the most important relations will be completely lost (eg, Tigers will file a long way away from Cats). Since the showing of relationships by juxtaposition is relatively poor, the display is dependent to a large extent on *references,* or *cross-references.*

These references are of two kinds:

1 those linking related subject headings under *both* of which entries for documents have been made

  in the form 'Subject X *see also* Subject Y'

2 those *leading* from subject headings which have been *rejected* for the purpose of document entry (but which the user may still think of consulting) *to* subject headings under which entries have been made

  in the form 'Subject X *see* Subject Y'

Chain procedure provides a systematic method of selecting *see* and *see also references* which will guide the searcher to the specific subject heading he desires and indicate related headings.

The user may well formulate his request at a more general, less specific level than that of the subject he actually requires. We encountered this when dealing with the classified catalogue.

For example, when searching for information about the subject *'Metallurgical assaying'* he may consult the catalogue under the term

'*Metallurgy*' while the specific subject he wants has been entered under the heading

    Assaying : Metallurgy

There is no classified sequence of subjects which will lead him from metallurgy to the sub-class *assaying : metallurgy* in the A/Z subject catalogue. We must provide him with a *see also* reference.

Chain procedure allows us to select a series of *see also* references from broader to narrower subjects ('general to special').

These are made <u>one step at a time</u> from *superordinate* to *subordinate* terms in the chain. This of course assumes that both terms are 'sought' terms.

In each case the lead term in the subject statements is qualified by the minimum number of superordinate terms necessary to indicate its *precise* context. If this qualification is *not* observed we will produce only *generalised* series of references—connections between *specific* headings will not be made.

To ensure that this does not occur write down the *full subject heading* corresponding to *each step in the chain*. Then construct your *see also* references from these headings, not from the single terms used in your initial analysis of the chain.

    Eg   *Subject*   '*Select methods of metallurgical assaying*'

	Class number	669.9		
	Chain	6	Technology	Technology
		66	Chemical	Chemical technology
		669	Metallurgy	Metallurgy
		669.9	Assaying	Assaying : Metallurgy

The specific subject heading for this subject is,

    Assaying : Metallurgy

We now make a series of see also references, one step at a time from broader to narrower subjects culminating in the specific subject heading thus:

Technology	*see also*	Chemical technology
Chemical technology	*see also*	Metallurgy
Metallurgy	*see also*	Assaying : Metallurgy

Now consider the following subject of a document entitled,

'*The role of higher education*'

Class number	378		
Chain	3	Social sciences	Social sciences
	37	Education	Education
	378	Higher	Higher education

    Specific subject heading   Higher education

Which of the following series of references is from broader to narrower subjects?

Higher education *see also* Education

Education   *see also* Social sciences   — frame 336

Social sciences   *see also* Education

Education   *see also* Higher education — frame 341

340 (323, 338)

Correct. The basic significance order referred to is

    Thing $\longrightarrow$ Material $\longrightarrow$ Action $\longrightarrow$ Agent

If we decide to *modify* the citation order prescribed by chain procedure to produce a subject heading regarded as more helpful to the catalogue user, then this *significance order* can be employed as a guide in determining the modified citation order.

Consider *'Notes on the diagnosis of occupational diseases'*. Let us suppose you classify this document by UDC as follows:

Class number	616-057-07	
Chain	6	Applied science
	61	Medicine
	616	Disease
	616-05	Environmental
	616-057	Occupational
	616-057-07	Diagnosis

If you produce a subject heading employing the significance order Thing $\longrightarrow$ Material $\longrightarrow$ Action $\longrightarrow$ Agent, which of the following headings would you arrive at?

    Diagnosis : Occupational diseases   – frame 345

    Occupational diseases : Diagnosis   – frame 324

341 (339)

Your answer: the following series of references leads from broader to narrower subjects:

     Social sciences   *see also* Education

     Education   *see also* Higher education

Correct. These have been constructed, *one step at a time,* from *superordinate* to *subordinate terms* in the chain. this has produced a series of *see also* references leading from broader to narrower subjects culminating in the specific subject heading

     Higher education

The making of a series of *see also* references from qualified *subordinate* to qualified *superordinate* terms in the chain, ie from *narrower* to *broader* subjects (*'special to general'*) is very simply done using the same chain structure.

     Eg

     Higher education *see also* Education

     Education   *see also* Social sciences

However, in most A/Z subject catalogues such references are omitted purely on grounds of economy.

In view of the frequency with which users could benefit from references to a broader subject this omission must be regarded as a deficiency of A/Z subject catalogues.

Continue on the next frame

See also references from subjects *related* to the specific subject *but not present in the chain structure of that subject* can also be helpful to the searcher.

Such related subjects may appear in fairly widely separated parts of the classification schedule however, eg,

Social geography *see also* Town planning

The selection of such references is very much at the discretion of the indexer and as yet no firm rules have been developed to guide him in his choice.

For the purposes of this course, you must concentrate on *see also* references derived from the conceptual chain of the specific subject, leading one step at a time from qualified superordinate to qualified subordinate terms. These are the traditionally used general to special references leading from broader to narrower subjects and culminating in the specific subject heading.

Continue on the next frame

343 (342)

We must finally consider the use of *see* references derived by chain procedure.

These are the references which direct the searcher *from rejected headings to the chosen headings* under which entries for documents have been made.

You will recall that time and form concepts are usually *suppressed* in a subject heading. Thus '*A dictionary of medicine*' would be entered under the heading

Medicine : Dictionaries

This is regarded as a more helpful subject heading than the one produced by strict adherence to the citation order prescribed by chain procedure, ie

Dictionaries : Medicine

We must still provide for the user who consults the catalogue under the terms representing form concepts however.

We make this provision by *blanket* or *general* references similar to those employed in the A/Z subject index to the classified catalogue, eg

Dictionaries on special subjects *see* Names of individual subjects,

eg Medicine : Dictionaries

'The same procedure is adopted for time concepts. Direct entry under a time concept is both wasteful and unhelpful in most subjects and thus we use a blanket reference, eg

History of individual subjects *see* Names of the individual subjects.

Continue on the next frame

In the A/Z subject catalogue entries for individual *documents* are made under the chosen subject heading.

It is thus uneconomical and wasteful of space in the catalogue to provide entries for documents under *all synonymous* subject headings.

Consequently the practice is to select one term as an indexing term, ie, to be used for document entry. The user is then referred *from* synonymous terms to the chosen term under which entries have been made.

For example, we might select *Cardiovascular system* as an indexing term for use in subject headings and reject the synonym *Circulatory system*.

We must then provide the following see reference for the benefit of the user who consults the catalogue under the rejected term:

Circulatory system *see* Cardiovascular system

You are already aware that the recognition of synonyms is one of the processes in editing a chain.

When synonyms occur, *see* references must be made *from* the rejected term, or terms, *to* the chosen indexing term.

A most important kind of *see* reference generated by chain procedure is that made from a *rejected specific subject heading* to the *chosen specific subject heading*.

If we modify the citation order prescribed by chain procedure when selecting the specific subject heading for a compound subject we, at the same time, *reject* a specific subject heading in the alternative, less helpful citation order, ie that one prescribed by strict adherence to chain procedure.

It is essential to direct the user *from* the rejected subject heading *to* the chosen subject heading. We do this by a *see* reference.

Consider a document about *'The diagnosis of diseases'*.

UDC class number	616-07	
Chain	6	Applied sciences
	61	Medicine
	616	Diseases
	616-07	Diagnosis

The chosen specific subject heading is *Diseases : Diagnosis*.

Having selected this heading, which of the following references would you employ?

Diseases : Diagnosis *see also* Diagnosis : Diseases — frame 325

Diagnosis : Diseases *see*   Diseases : Diagnosis — frame 337

Your answer
>Diagnosis : Occupational diseases.

No, this is a wrong decision.

In this compound subject the concept 'Diagnosis' is an *Action* performed on 'Occupational diseases'.

Therefore your citation order does *not* follow the basic significance order
>Thing → Material → Action → Agent

Please return to frame 340. Read again about the *modification* of chain procedure order, look carefully at the example, then select the correct answer to the question and proceed with the course.

Your answer:

     Abolition : Slavery *see* Slavery : Abolition

Correct.

We have modified chain procedure order to produce the heading Slavery Abolition. We must therefore provide the *see reference* from the rejected form of heading. This ensures that the sought term in the chain, Abolition, occupies the *lead position* in a reference.

In this instance we have also modified chain procedure order to produce the *specific subject heading*

     Slavery : Abolition : USA

The *space* concept has been suppressed in the heading. In many subjects space is thus suppressed in specific subject headings although this is not such a general rule as the suppression of form or time. In some subjects, eg History, Geography, space occupies a primary role and entry under these concepts may well be helpful. This may also apply in certain of the Social sciences and entry under space is very much at the discretion of the indexer

However, the modifications to chain procedure order decided upon in this example, might lead the indexer to make the following references.

     Slavery   *see also*   Slavery : Abolition

     Slavery : Abolition   *see also*   Slavery : Abolition : USA

Having once directed the user to the heading *Slavery* it is reasonable to expect him to search *all* the entries under this term and its subheadings.

Consequently these two references would usually be omitted. They would only be provided if the number of entries filed under Slavery and its subheadings was very large.

We should, of course, still require the see reference from the rejected specific subject heading.

     USA : Slavery : Abolition   *see*   Slavery : Abolition : USA

Let us look finally at the edited chain and the specific subject heading and references derived from it.

Subject	'The abolition of slavery in the USA'		
Class no	326.8 (73)		
Chain	3	Social sciences	Social sciences
	32	Political science=Politics	Political science
	326	Slavery	Slavery
	326.8	Abolition	Slavery : Abolition
	326.8(7/8)	(Americas)	
	326.8(7)	(North America)	
	326.8	USA=United States of America	Slavery : Abolition : USA

Specific subject heading   Slavery : Abolition : USA
References

Social sciences	*see also*	Political science
Political science	*see also*	Slavery
Abolition : Slavery	*see*	Slavery : Abolition
USA : Slavery : Abolition	*see*	Slavery : Abolition : USA
Politics	*see*	Political science
United States of America	*see*	USA

The guiding principle is always that the system of *see* and *see also* references directs the user to the specific subject heading chosen for the subject.
Continue on the next frame

347   (346)

Chain procedure, or, more precisely, *modified chain procedure,* is by no means the *only* method of deriving subject headings and references for the A/Z subject catalogue. It is, however, the one examined for the purposes of this course and it does provide a systematic method of:

1 Selecting a subject heading which is a *specific description* of the document's summarised subject content;

2 economically generating a series of *see* and *see also* references which lead the user to this specific subject heading by providing an entry point in the catalogue for each term in the chain reflecting the different hierarchical levels of a user's approach to the subject.

We shall now briefly summarise the main points regarding modified chain procedure and then you will be required to employ this method for yourself.

SUMMARY

1 Having classified a document, analyse the class assigned into its complete conceptual chain and edit this chain as required.

2 Write down the *full subject heading* corresponding to each sought link in this edited chain.

3 Construct the *specific subject heading* by leading with the last term in th chain, qualified by the minimum number of superordinate terms.

4 *Modify* this order *only* if you think that, by doing so, you produce a more helpful specific subject heading.

5 When modifying chain procedure order use the *basic significance order* Thing → Material → Action → Agent as your guide.

6 These last two points apply equally to the selecting of subject headings corresponding to superordinate steps in the chain.

7 Construct a series of *see also* references leading *one step at a time* from broader to narrower subjects and culminating in the chosen specific subject heading.

8 Construct *see* references from *synonyms* and from *rejected forms of com pound subject headings.*

9 Check to ensure that the system of references directs the user to the chosen specific subject heading and that all *sought terms* in the chain appea as lead terms in this system of references.

Continue on the next frame

Having now concluded out consideration of the A/Z subject catalogue, we suggest that you try the following exercise in applying modified chain procedure to the construction subject headings and references.

Earlier in the course you provided a subject analysis and a UDC class number for each of the following examples. These are repeated here for convenience.

1 *'Therapy through hypnosis'*
    SA   Medicine/Therapeutics/Hypnotherapy
    UDC 615.851.2

2 *'Roots of contemporary American architecture: a series of essays'*
    SA   Architecture/Contemporary/American/Essays
    UDC 72.036(73)(04)

For each of the above subjects would you now produce:

a) an analysis of the chain
b) a specific subject heading and a series of subject references by modified chain procedure

Check your answers with those provided on frame 355.

COLON CLASSIFICATION: Categories and citation order in 6th ed
(Classes arranged in UDC order for comparison and aid in using UDC)

UDC	Class	CC	Canonical divisions	Systems	Specials	P₁	P₂	P₃	P₄	M	E	2P	2P₂	2E	3P
02	Library science	2				Libraries				Stock	Operations				
1	Philosophy	R	Logics, Ethics, etc												
159.9	Psychology	S		Gestalt		Persons					Mental processes			Anatomy, Pathology, etc	
2	Religion	Q				Religions					Beliefs and practices				
248.2	Mysticism	△				Religions	God, Devil, Man, etc				Techniques				
30	Sociology	Y				Groups					Activities	Activities		Treatment of social problems	
311	Statistics	B28				Form of state	Offices of state								
32	Political science	W									Practices, policies, and problems				
33+38 & 65	Economics	X		Communism, etc	Scale	Business					Activities				
34	Law	Z				Legal system	Subjects of law								
35	Public administration		This subject distributed in Colon classes V, X, M and L												

UDC	Class	CC	Canonical divisions	Systems	Specials	P₁	P₂	P₃	P₄	M	E	2P	2P₂	2E	3P
36	Social work	YX	No schedule given in Colon. Assume similar structure to Y												
37	Education			Montessori, etc		Stages					Activities	Subject taught	Methods and taught aids	Methods	Treatment of social problems
39	Social anthropology	Y7									Activities				
4	Linguistics	P				Groups, Language variants	Stage elements				Structure and analysis				
502	Natural history		This subject distributed in Colon at G:12, I:12, K:12.												
51	Mathematics	B	Arithmetic, algebra, etc			Differential treatment within canonical divisions									
52	Astronomy	B9				Heavenly body					Orbits, eclipses, etc				
53	Physics	C	Heat, Light, etc			Differential treatment within canonical divisions									
531/533	Mechanics	B7				State of matter					Process				
54	Chemistry	H1				Substance					Process				
548	Mineralogy	H				Substance					Operations				
55	Earth sciences (Geology, etc)	H	Petrology, etc			Differential treatment within canonical divisions									
56	Paleontology	H6				Fossils									
571	Archaeology	V:71 (distributed class by country)													

UDC	Class	CC	Canonical divisions	Systems	Specials	P1	P2	P3	P4	M	E	2P	2P2	2E	3P
572	Physical anthropology	Y7:2				Race									
574	Biology	G			Stage of growth	Organ					Processes				
58	Botany	I				Plant	Organ				Processes				
59	Zoology	K				Animal	Organ				Processes				
61	Medicine	L		Homeopathy, etc	Stage of growth, etc	Organ					Processes				Treatment of diseases
62	Engineering	D				Civil, Mechanical, etc	Part			Material	Operations				
622	Mining	HX				Substance	Plant and equipment								
63	Agriculture	J		Forestry, etc	Soil-less farming, etc	Crop	Organ				Operations			Treatment of diseases, etc	
636/639	Animal husbandry	KX				Animal					Operations			Treatment of diseases, etc	
64	Domestic	MA				Cooking, etc					Operations				
66/67	Chemical technology	F				Product					Operations				
67/68	Useful arts	M	Various crafts			Product					Operations				

UDC	Class	CC	Canonical divisions	Systems	Specials	P₁	P₂	P₃	P₄	M	E	2P	2P₂	2E	3P
69	Building	D3				Kind of building	Part of building			Material	Operations				
7	Fine arts	N	Various arts			Style———(for all arts)									
71	Town planning	NB				"	"	Kind of town	Part of town		Operations				
72	Architecture	NA				"	"	Kind of building	Part of building		Operations				
73/76	Sculpture, painting, etc	ND, etc				"	"	Subject		Material	Operations				
77	Photography	M95														
78	Music	NR				Style		Form etc		Instruments	Technique				
791/795	Entertainment (drama, cinema, etc)	NS/NW														
796/799	Sports	MY				Various sports										
8	Literature	O				Language	Form	Author	Work		Criticism				
91	Geography	U				Physical, economic, etc										
92	Biography	W														
93	History	V				Country	Offices of state				Activities				

353 (268)

Answers to the examples set in frame 268.

1 *'Library resources in the Greater London area: No 5 Agricultural libraries'*
   SA   Library science/Special libraries/Agriculture/London
   UDC 026:63(421)

2 *'Therapy through hypnosis'*
   SA   Medicine/Therapeutics/Hypnotherapy
   UDC 615.851.2

This class number is enumerated for you in the index although it does not occur in the schedules of the abridged UDC (see the index entry Hypnc and then its subheading psychotherapy). This is, therefore, an instance where the index provides you with a more specific class number than is enumerated at the appropriate part of the abridged schedules themselves. The class number so provided in such cases is correct and should be used.

However, if you have consulted the index under the entry for, say, Psychotherapy itself, you will only have the lead to class 615.851. If you have then constructed a compound class number by sub-dividing 615.851 by the concept hypnotism you should have arrived at
    615.851:159.962

3 *'Cereal diseases: Ministry of Agriculture, Fisheries and Food Bulletin No 129'*
   SA   Agriculture/Cereals/Diseases
   UDC 633.1-2

4 *'Roots of contemporary American architecture: a series of essays*
   SA   Architecture/American/Contemporary/Essays
   UDC 72.03(73)6(04)

In this discipline Space and Time together form the Style facet and, as such, constitute 'Personality' concepts. The above citation order is achieved by the intercalation of (73). You may well have employed the citation order
    Architecture/Contemporary/American/Essays
where Time precedes space in the formation of the Style facet. Translated, this citation order gives the UDC class number
    72.036(73)(04)

5 *'The selected poems of Robert Graves'*
   SA   Literature/English/Poetry/Robert Graves/Selections
   UDC 820-1 Graves 3

§

We hope that, if your answers diverged from the above solutions, you are able to appreciate why the divergence occurred.

A potential area of difference is obviously in the choice of citation order. In UDC there is no 'correct' citation order. Thus, when providing instruction in the use of the scheme, it is necessary to conform to some guiding principle in this choice. We have employed PME...ST as just such a general guide. We do not imply that this citation order is the one that should be used in relation to UDC in all contexts. The important point to appreciate is that the indexer must decide on a citation order and adhere to it when classifying by UDC.

Your knowledge of and practice in the use of UDC will form the basis for the remainder of this course and so, if you think there are parts of these first two sections you ought to revise, this is the time to do it. Resume the course on frame 269.

354 (321)

Answers to the examples set on frame 321.

1 *'Cereal diseases: Ministry of Agriculture, Fisheries and Food Bulletin No 129'*

SA   Agriculture/Cereals/Diseases

UDC   633.1-2

Chain   6   Applied sciences
             63   Agriculture
             633   Crops
             633.1   Cereals
             633.1-2 Diseases

A/Z subject index entries

Diseases : Cereals : Agriculture	633.1-2
Cereals : Agriculture	633.1
Crops : Agriculture	633
Agriculture	63
Applied sciences	6

2 *'Library resources in the Greater London area: No 5 Agricultural libraries'*

SA   Library science/Special libraries/Agriculture/London

UDC   026:63(421)

Chain   0   (Generalities)
             02   Librarianship=Library science. Libraries
             026   Special libraries
             026:6   (Applied sciences)
             026:63   Agriculture
             *026:63(4)   Europe
             *026:63(41-4) UK
             *026:63(420) England
             026:63(421) London

A/Z subject index entries

London : Agricultural libraries	026:63(421)
Agricultural libraries	026:63
Special libraries	026
Libraries	02
Librarianship	02
Library science	02

*whether or not to make entries under England, UK and Europe is at the discretion of the indexer. In many situations they would probably be regarded as unnecessary.

Please proceed with the course on frame 322.

Answers to examples set on frame 348.

1 *'Theraphy through hypnosis'*

SA	Medicine/Therapeutics/Hypnotherapy		
UDC	615.851.2		
Chain	6	Applied sciences	Applied sciences
	61	Medicine=Medical sciences	Medicine
	615	Therapeutics	Therapeutics : Medicine
	615.8	(Physiotheraphy)	
	615.85	(Various treatments)	
	615.851	Psychotherapy	Psychotherapy
	615.851.2	Hypnotherapy	Hypnotherapy

Subject heading   Hypnotherapy

References

Applied sciences	*see also*	Medicine
Medicine	*see also*	Therapeutics : Medicine
Therapeutics : Medicine	*see also*	Psychotherapy
Psychotherapy	*see also*	Hypnotherapy
Medical sciences	*see*	Medicine

2 *'Roots of contemporary American architecture: a series of essays'*

SA	Architecture/Contemporary/American/Essays		
UDC	72.036(73)(04)		
Chain	7	Arts=Fine arts	Fine arts
	72	Architecture	Architecture
	72.03	(Style)	
	72.036	Contemporary=Modern	Contemporary architecture
	72.036(7/8)	(The Americas)	
	72.036(7)	(North America)	
	72.036(73)	USA=United States of America	USA : Contemporary architecture
	72.036(73)(04)	Essays	

Subject heading   USA : Contemporary architecture : Essays

References

Fine arts	*see also*	Architecture
Architecture	*see also*	Contemporary architecture
Contemporary architecture	*see also*	USA: Contemporary architecture
Essays		General reference
Modern architecture	*see*	Contemporary architecture
United States of America	*see*	USA

Please continue on frame 357.

356 (357)

Answers to examples set on frame 357.

1 *'Teachers in higher education in the United Kingdom: an official report'*

    SA   Education/Higher/Teachers/UK/Report

    UDC   378.12 (41-4) (047)

    Chain 3   Social sciences

              37   Education

              378   Higher

              378.1   (General organisation)

              378.12   Teachers

              378. 12(41-4)   UK=United Kingdom

              378.12(41-4)(047) Reports

  A/Z subject index entries

        Reports   General reference

        UK : Teachers : Higher education   378.12(41-4)

        Teachers : Higher education   378.12

        Higher education   378

        Education   37

        Social sciences   3

        United Kingdom *see* UK

2 *'The education of women in India: a bibliography'*

    SA   Education/Women/India/Bibliography

    UDC   371.04-055.2(540):016

    Chain 3   Social sciences   Social sciences

              37   Education   Education

              371   (Teaching etc)

              371.04   (with reference to pupil)

              371.04-055.2   Women   Women : Education

              371.04-055.2(540) India   India : Women :
                                           Education

              371.04-055.2(540):016 Bibliographies India : Women
                                               Education :
                                               Bibliographies

  Subject heading India : Women : Education : Bibliographies

  References

             Bibliographies   General reference

        Social sciences   *see also* Education

        Education   *see also* Women : Education

        Women : Education *see also* India : Women : Education

You have now completed this volume which has been concerned with the UDC, the classified catalogue and the A/Z subject catalogue.

The objectives of this part of the course could be stated in the following terms:

Having produced a specific summarisation of the subject content of a document cast in PME...ST citation order, you should be able

1 to translate this subject analysis into a UDC class number following your citation order as far as the scheme allows.

2 to produce entries for this subject, by chain indexing procedure, for the A/Z subject index to a single entry system classified catalogue employing UDC.

3 to produce, by modified chain procedure based on UDC, a specific subject heading and a system of references for this subject in an A/Z subject catalogue.

Such a statement of objectives may appear narrowly defined in its practices and yet, at the same time, rather sweeping in its assumptions. Some amplification is therefore desirable to place it in its full context.

It was not our aim, nor indeed is it feasible in a course of this nature, to make the reader highly proficient in all aspects of classification with UDC and in all methods employable in the construction of subject catalogues. We selected certain procedures, the appreciation of which we consider of fundamental importance in understanding the use of classification schemes and the structure of subject catalogues. On the other hand, to claim total competence in the application of even these selected skills to all subjects expressable in documents obviously requires a breadth of knowledge and a degree of practice lying far beyond the capabilities of a course such as this to inculcate.

These objectives should thus be viewed as part of the wider intent of the course. Through practice in these particular procedures, we have attempted to acquaint you with a set of basic principles that will help you to classify documents and produce entries in subject catalogues with an awareness of the structure and limitations of the tools you are using, an appreciation of your ultimate objective and thus an ability to obtain this end more efficiently.

As a concluding exercise we suggest you apply the *total* process of subject analysis, classification by UDC and the provision of catalogue entries by chain procedure to each of the two following examples:

1 *'Teachers in higher education in the United Kingdom: an official report'*

2 *'The education of women in India: a bibliography'*

For both these examples produce
- a) a subject analysis at the level of specific summarisation, cast in a PME...ST citation order.
- b) a UDC class number following your citation order as far as the scheme allows.

For the subject of example 1, produce a series of entries for an A/Z subject index to a classified catalogue by chain indexing procedure.

For the subject of example 2, produce a specific subject heading and a system reference as for the A/Z subject catalogue, by modified chain procedure.

Check your answers with the solutions suggested on frame 356.

INDEX TO VOLUMES I AND II

The frame numbers given indicate where a concept is first introduced. When appropriate, a subsequent treatment of the concept is also indicated.